THE SPIRITUAL LIFE

Cover art and design by
Carol W. Wells

THE SPIRITUAL LIFE

ANNIE BESANT

*This publication made possible with
the assistance of the Kern Foundation*

The Theosophical Publishing House

Wheaton, Ill. U.S.A.
Madras, India/London, England

The Theosophical Publishing House
P.O. Box 270
Wheaton, IL 60189-0270

A publication of the Theosophical Publishing House,
a department of The Theosophical Society in America

Library of Congress Cataloging-in Publication Data

Besant, Annie Wood, 1847-1933.
    The spiritual life / Annie Besant.
    p. cm.
    ISBN 0-8356-0666-X (pbk.) : $8.95
    1. Theosophy.   2. Spiritual life.   I. Title.
BP563.S65 1991
299'.934—dc20   90-50586
                                                       CIP

Printed in the United States of America

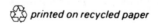 *printed on recycled paper*

Contents

Foreword
Joy Mills

When Annie Wood Besant joined the Theosophical Society in 1889—following a reading of the newly published volumes of *The Secret Doctrine* by H. P. Blavatsky, and a memorable meeting with their author—she had already achieved fame if not fortune in her native England. Any survey of her life (1847-1933) must take into account her numerous "lives," to draw on one biographer's description of the stages of her progress in thought (Prof. Arthur Nethercot). She had become, in turn, agnostic, theist, atheist, socialist, reformer, advocate of women's rights and the rights of workers. At the age of forty-two, when she came to Theosophy, she had accomplished far more than many, whether man or woman, had achieved in a lifetime. Her associate in the socialist cause, George Bernard Shaw, hailed her as the greatest orator of her day.

Yet her life and work from that memorable date of her affiliation with the Theosophical Society to the end of the incarnation were to be even more multifaceted than the preceding years. She was immediately plunged into lecturing for the Society and swiftly rose to a position of leadership, eventually becoming its President on the death of Col. H. S. Olcott in 1907. The brilliance of her lectures and writings, her magnetic personality, combined with her exceptional administrative skills, resulted in attracting thousands to the causes she espoused, the principal one being that of the Society itself. Her role in the home rule for India movement, her work in establishing schools and colleges in India and fostering educational reform everywhere, her adoption of the young boy, J. Krishnamurti, and her subsequent announcements of the role he would play as a world teacher, are all legendary. She was tireless in service, for to her the theosophical philosophy was meant to be practical, to speak to the human condition and the conditions of life itself in all its multitude of forms. She was a feminist before the movement for women's rights was fully launched; she was an environmentalist before ecology became a household word; she stood for freedom when half the world was held in the bonds of colonialism.

Through all her work, however, there flowed a single stream of thought, a concern for the inner life. In her childhood, as she remarked in her autobiography, this took the form of a deep mystical consciousness, an awareness of something inwardly present in the secret places of one's being. In her adult years, this sense of the mystical took on other guises, and within theosophical thought she found a new focus for its expression. At the time she came to the Society, she was immersed in the materialistic view so prevalent in the latter part of the nineteenth century, a view not wholly out of mode today. The theosophical vision of human nature, however, unfolded before her the realization that there are spiritual dimensions of our nature, dimensions that underlie the material expression in physical form. This was a vision she grasped at once, recognizing its validity both for its practical applications in our lives and for the promise it held for our future growth and development. Now it was the spiritual welfare of humanity that absorbed her attention, as much if not more than the physical and intellectual welfare of her fellow beings.

The present collection of some of her writings and lectures gives ample evidence of that primary concern for the inner life of the individual and of her recognition that consciousness must be changed from within if outer conditions are to be improved. The re-issuance of this work, first published nearly seven decades ago, marks Annie Besant's writings in this field as being just as relevant today as they were when she first wrote and spoke them. In spite of the numerous movements spawned by what has been called the "new age" or the "age of Aquarius," humanity still hungers for meaningfulness, for an understanding of the deeper truths of those areas of life to which the term "spiritual" generally refers. Above all, the question is still asked: Can we live and work in the world as it is, and at the same time lead a spiritual and therefore meaningful life? And, as a corollary: Is there a way of life, an ethic, which aids us in our quest for wisdom? Dr. Besant's answers to these questions, as well as to similar ones that arise in the earnest student's mind, speak to us today as they did to her audiences of an earlier period. When answers come from a heart overflowing with compassion for the sufferings of humankind, when they flow from a wisdom tradition that is timeless in its essence, then those answers are timeless, for they remind us that within us is the very truth we seek.

A number of the chapters were lectures given by Dr. Besant in various times and places. A majority of the chapters are drawn from the magazine which she edited with her colleague, the great classic scholar. G. R. S. Mead. That journal, *The Theosophical Review*, published in London, had formerly been known as *Lucifer*, a journal begun and edited by H. P. Blavatsky, but renamed by Besant because of the unhappy connotations many of her day were attributing to its original name. Yet true to its original name, the journal under Besant and Mead was still a "light-bearer," as Besant herself was a transmitter of light to the countless thousands whose lives she touched.

Two of the chapters in this work deserve special attention. Chapters IX and X were talks which Besant delivered at the Parliament of World Religions, that unique congress held in conjunction with the Columbian World's Fair in Chicago in 1893. The then President of the Theosophical Society, Col. H. S. Olcott, had deputed William Q. Judge, head of the Society's American Section, to represent him officially, and had sent Annie Besant as "special delegate" to speak on behalf of the Society. So brilliant were her talks that the halls which had been assigned to the Society for the occasion were filled to overflowing, and Dr. Jerome Anderson, editor of the *Pacific Theosophist,* in reporting on her lectures, remarked that "Seldom has a [greater] tide of eloquence ever flowed from human lips than came from those of Annie Besant." Discussing the meaning of altruism, Besant sounded a keynote as essential for our lives today as it has always been: that our supreme duty is to follow the universal law of life, the service of humanity. Especially relevant today are the closing words of the second of her addresses at the Parliament: ". . . no nation can endure whose foundations are not divine. . . . Yours is the choice, and as you express it the America of centuries to come will bless you for your living, or will condemn you for your failure; for you are the creators of the world, and as you will so it shall be."

If today we stand on the threshold of a new world order, out of conflict and violence envisioning a world of beauty and of peace, then this book can awaken us to our responsibilities as creators of such a world. It can encourage us to live the kind of life, spiritually based and inwardly directed, that will ensure that harmony among peoples and among nations may prevail.

Publisher's Preface
To the New Edition

The words in the talks and articles that comprise this work were uttered or written seventy or more years ago by a woman from the Victorian era. Obviously, styles of expression have changed drastically since then, and today's readers may have difficulty absorbing the thoughts cast in such language. Therefore, in order to make Annie Besant's messages more accessible today, we have updated the text somewhat while making every effort to remain true to its spirit and meaning.

We have broken down lengthy sentences and paragraphs, eliminated or modified outdated words and expressions, eliminated citations from persons known in Besant's time but now forgotten. After much thought we decided to change the language to be inclusive, in keeping with modern usage. Therefore, we have substituted such terms as "humanity" and "humankind" for "man," eliminated "he" and "him" when they mean anyone or everyone, and generally replaced masculine pronouns when appropriate. Annie Besant was an early feminist, and we feel that this is how she would express herself today.

We hope readers will be better able to respond to Annie Besant's inspiring ideas in this form, for they are both timeless and pertinent to today's world.

Original
Publisher's Preface

A new school of thought is arising to challenge long-accepted views of life. Its keynote may be said to be "evolutionary creation." It is an exposition of the phenomena that surround us in terms that are both scientific and idealistic. It offers an explanation of life, of the origin of our fragment of the universe, of hidden and mysterious natural laws, of the nature and destiny of man, that appeals with moving force to the logical mind. This school of thought is at the same time both iconoclastic and constructive, for it is sweeping away old dogmas that are no longer tenable in the light of rapidly developing modern science, while it is building a substantial structure of facts beneath the age-long dream of immortality.

The literature that is growing out of ideas which are so revolutionary in the intellectual realm and yet are so welcome to a world groping through the fogs of materialism, is receiving a warm welcome in other lands, and it should be better known here.

In addition to the large number of volumes which stand in the name of Annie Besant, there is a great quantity of literature, for which she is responsible, that has appeared in more fugitive form as articles, pamphlets and published lectures, issued not only in America, but in Great Britain, India and Australia. Much of this work is of great interest, but is quite out of reach of the general reader as it is no longer in print, and inquiries for many such items have frequently to be answered in the negative. Under these circumstances The

Theosophical Press decided to issue an edition of Mrs. Besant's collected writings under the title, *The Spiritual Life.*

The importance and interest of such a collection of essays, both as supplementing treatment of many of the topics in larger works and as affording expression of the author's views on many subjects not otherwise dealt with, will be obvious, and it only remains to express the publishers' hope that the convenience and moderate cost of the series may insure its thorough circulation among the wide range of Mrs. Besant's readers.

1

The Spiritual Life in the World

A complaint which we hear continually from thoughtful and earnest-minded people, a complaint against the circumstances of their lives, is perhaps one of the most fatal: "If my circumstances were different from what they are, how much more I could do; if only I were not so surrounded by business, so tied by anxieties and cares, so occupied with the work of the world, then I would be able to live a more spiritual life."

Now that is not true. No circumstances can ever make or mar the unfolding of the spiritual life. Spirituality does not depend upon the environment; it depends upon one's attitude towards life.

I want to point out to you the way in which the world may be turned to the service of the spirit instead of submerging it, as it often does. If people do not understand the relation of the material and the spiritual; if they separate the one from the other as incompatible and hostile; if on the one side they put the life of the world, and on the other the life of the spirit as rivals, as antagonists, as enemies, then the pressing nature of worldly occupations, the powerful shocks of the material environment, the constant lure of physical temptation, and the occupying of the brain by physical cares —these things are apt to make the life of the spirit unreal. They seem to be the only reality, and we have to find some alchemy, some magic, by which the life of the world shall be seen to be the unreal, and the life of the spirit the only reality. If we can do that, then the reality will express itself through the life of the world, and that life will become its

1

means of expression, and not a bandage round its eyes, a gag which stops the breath.

Now, you know how often in the past this question of whether a person can lead a spiritual life in the world has been answered in the negative. In every land, in every religion, in every age of the world's history, when the question has been asked, the answer has been no, the man or woman of the world cannot lead a spiritual life. That answer comes from the deserts of Egypt, the jungles of India, the monastery and the nunnery in Roman Catholic countries, in every land and place where people have sought to find God by shrinking from the company of others. If for the knowledge of God and the leading of the spiritual life it is necessary to fly from human haunts, then that life for most of us is impossible. For we are bound by circumstance that we cannot break to live the life of the world and to accommodate ourselves to its conditions separating the sacred from the profane.

I submit to you that this idea is based on a fundamental error that is largely fostered in our modern life, not by thinking of secluded life in jungle or desert, in cave or monastery, but rather by thinking that the religious and the secular must be kept apart. That tendency is because of the modern way of separating the so-called sacred from that which is called profane. People speak of Sunday as the Lord's Day, as though every day were not equally for serving him. To call one day the Lord's Day is to deny that same lordship to every other day in the week and to make six parts of life outside the spiritual, while only one remains recognized as dedicated to the Spirit. And so common talk of sacred history and profane history, religious education and secular education, all these phrases that are so commonly used, hypnotize the public mind into a false view of the Spirit and the world. The right way is to say that the Spirit is the life, the world the form, and the form must be the expression of the life; otherwise you have a corpse devoid of life, an unembodied life separated from all means of effective action.

I want to put broadly and strongly the very foundation of

what I believe to be right and sane thinking in this matter. The world is the thought of God, the expression of the Divine Mind. All useful activities are forms of Divine Activity. The wheels of the world are turned by God, and we are only his hands, which touch the rim of the wheel. All work done in the world is God's work, or none is his at all. Everything that serves humanity and helps in the activities of the world is rightly seen as a divine activity, and wrongly seen when called secular or profane. The clerk behind his counter and the doctor in the hospital are quite as much engaged in a divine activity as any preacher in his church. Until that is realized the world is vulgarized, and until we can see one life everywhere and all things rooted in that life, it is we who are hopelessly profane in attitude, we who are blind to the beatific vision which is the sight of the one life in everything, and all things as expressions of that life.

Divinity Everywhere

An ancient Indian scripture says, "I established this universe with one fragment of Myself, and I remain." Now, if there is only one life in which you and I are partakers, one creative thought by which the worlds were formed and maintained, then, however mighty may be the unexpressed Divine Existence—however true that Divinity transcends manifestation, nonetheless the manifestation is still divine. By understanding this we touch the feet of God. If it is true that he is everywhere and in everything, then he is as much in the marketplace as in the desert, as much in the office as in the jungle, as easily found in the street of the crowded city as in the solitude of the mountain peak.

I do not mean that it is not easier for you and for me to realize the divine greatness in the splendor of snow-clad mountains, the beauty of some pine forest, the depth of some marvelous secret valley where Nature speaks in a voice that may be heard. I mean that although we hear more clearly there, it is because we are deaf, and not because the Divine Voice does not speak.

It is our weakness that the rush and the bustle of life in the city make us deaf to the Voice that is ever speaking. If we were stronger, if our ears were keener, if we were more spiritual, then we could find the Divine Life as readily in the rush of Holborn Viaduct as in the fairest scene that Nature has ever painted in the solitude of the mountain or the magic of the midnight sky. That is the first thing to realize —that we do not find because our eyes are blinded.

Worldly Attractions

Now let us see what are the conditions by which the man or woman of the world may lead the spiritual life, for there are conditions. Have you ever asked yourself why objects that attract you, things you want to possess are found on every side? Your desires answer to the outer beauty, the attractiveness of the endless objects that are scattered over the world. If they were not meant to attract, they would not be there; if they were really hindrances, why should they have been put in our path? For the same reasons that a mother, wanting to coax her child into the exertion that will induce it to walk, dangles before its eyes a little out of reach some dazzling toy, some tinsel attraction. The child's eyes turn to the brilliant object, and the child wants to grasp it. He tries to get on his feet, falls, and rises again, endeavors to walk, struggles to reach it. The value of the attraction is not in the tinsel that presently the child grasps, crushes, and throws away, wanting something more, but in the stimulus to the life within, which makes him endeavor to move in order to gain the glittering prize, which he despises when he has won it.

The great mother-heart by which we are trained is ever dangling in front of us some attractive object, some prize for the child-spirit, turning outwards the powers that live within. In order to induce exertion, in order to make the effort by which alone those inward-turned powers will turn outwards into manifestation, we are bribed and coaxed and induced to make efforts by the endless toys of life scattered on every side. We struggle, we endeavor to grasp. At last we do grasp and hold. After a short time the brilliant apple turns to ashes, as in Milton's fable, and the prize that seemed so valuable loses all its attractiveness, becomes worthless, and something else is desired. In that way we grow. The result is in ourselves; some power has been brought out, some faculty has been developed, some inner strength has become a manifested power, some hidden capacity has become faculty in action. That is the object of the Divine Teacher. The toy is thrown aside when the result of the exertion to gain it has been achieved.

So we pass from one point to another, from one stage of evolution to the next. Although until you believe in the great fact of continual rebirth and ever-continuing experience, you will not realize to the full the beauty and the splendor of the Divine Plan, still, even in one brief life you know you gain by your struggle and not by your accomplishment, and the reward of the struggle is in the power that you possess. In the words of Edward Carpenter, nineteenth-century English author, limited in scope if you do not believe in reincarnation, "Every pain that I suffered in one body was a power that I wielded in the next." Even in one brief span from the cradle to the grave you can trace the working of the law. You grow, not by what you gain of outer fruit, but by the inner unfolding necessary for your success in the struggle.

Lessons from the Worldly Life

Now, if long natural experience has made one wise, these objects lose their power to attract. The first tendency then is to cease from effort; but that would mean stagnation. When the objects of the world are becoming a little less valuable than they were, then is the time to look for some new motive. The motive to action for the spiritual life is, first, to perform action because it is duty, and not in order to gain the personal reward that it may bring. Let me take the case of a man [or woman] of the world and a spiritual person and see what is needed to turn one into the other. I take as example a man of the world, a man who is making some enormous fortune, who puts money before himself as the one object of life to be rich. It is a common thing.

Now, for a moment, pause on the life of the man who is determined to be rich. Everything is subordinated to that one aim. He must be master of his body, for if that body is his master, every week and month he will waste the money that he has gathered by struggle. He will waste it in luxury for the pleasing of the body, the money that he ought to grasp, in order to win more. And so the first thing that such a man must do is to master the body, to teach it to endure hardness, to learn to bear frugality, to learn to bear hardship even; not to think whether he wants to sleep, if by traveling all night a contract can be gained; not to stop to ask whether he shall rest if, by going to some party at midnight, he can make a friend who will enable him to gain more money by his influence. Over and over again in the struggle for gold the man must be master of this outer body that he wears, until it has no voice in determining his line of activity. It yields itself obedient servant to the dominant will, to the compelling brain. The first thing he learns is conquest of the body.

Then he learns concentration of mind. If he is not concentrated, his rivals will beat him in the struggle of the marketplace. If his mind wanders about here, there, and everywhere, undecided, one day trying one plan, another day another plan, without perseverance, without deliberate, continuing labor, that man will fail. The goal he desires teaches him to concentrate his mind; he brings it to one point; he holds it there as long as he needs to; he is steady in his persevering mental effort, and his mind grows stronger and stronger, keener and keener, more and more under his control. He has not only learned to control his body, but to control his mind.

Has he gained anything more? Yes, a strong will; only the strong will can succeed in such a struggle. The soul grows mighty in the attempt to achieve. Presently that man, with his mastered body, his well-controlled mind, his powerful will, gains his object and grasps his gold. And then? Then he finds out that, after all, he cannot do so very much with it to make happiness for himself; that he has only one body to clothe, one mouth to feed; that he cannot multiply his wants with the enormous supply that he can gain, and that, after all, his power to gain happiness is very limited.

His gold becomes a burden rather than a joy. The first delight of the achievement of his object palls, and he becomes satiated with possession, until in many cases he can do nothing but, by mere habit, roll and roll up increasing piles of useless gold. It becomes a nightmare rather than a delight; it crushes the man who won it.

Now, what will make that man a spiritual person? A change of his object—that is all. Let that man in this or any other life awaken to the valuelessness of the gold that he has heaped together; let him see the beauty of human service; let him catch a glimpse of the splendor of the Divine Order. Let him realize that all in life that is worthwhile is to give it as part of the great life by which the worlds are maintained.

The power that man has gained over body, over mind, over will, will make him a giant in the spiritual world. He does not need to change those qualities, but to get rid of the selfishness, of the indifference to human pain, of the recklessness with which he crushed his brother in order that he might climb into wealth on the starvation of myriads. He must change his ideal from selfishness to service; from strength used for crushing to strength used for uplifting. In the giant of the money market you will have the spiritual person. His life is consecrated to humanity, and he owns only to serve and to help. Difference of object, difference of motive—whether a man is of the world worldly or of the spirit spiritual depends on these, not difference of the outer life.

Changing Motives

I just now used the word "duty," for that is the first step. It does not matter what your work in the world may be if you begin to do it, not because it brings you a livelihood— though there is nothing to be ashamed of in that—but slowly, gradually, more and more you do it because it ought to be done, not because you want to gain something for yourself. Then you are taking the first step towards the spiritual life, you are changing your motive; all the activities of your day will have a new object.

Duty must be done; the wheels of the world must be kept

turning. Men and women must be fed along the various lines of trade and commerce; the sick must be healed; the ignorant must be taught; justice must be sought between the strong and the weak, and the rich and the poor. Looking at it thus, the tradesman, the merchant, the doctor, the lawyer, the teacher may all take a new view of life, and they may say: This activity with which I am engaged is part of the great working of the world which is divine. I am in it to do this work and my duty lies in the perfect performance of my task. I will teach, or heal, or argue, or trade, or enter into commercial relations of all kinds, not for the mere money that it brings or the power that it yields, but in order that the great work of the world may be worthily carried on; and that work may be done by me as servant of a will greater than my own, instead of for my own personal gain and profit.

That is the first step, and there is not one person that cannot take it. You may do your business just the same, but you carry a new spirit into it. You do it because it is your work in the world, as a servant does a task for his master because he is bidden to do it, and his loyalty makes him do it well. Then every addition of a number of figures in a ledger, every sale of an article in a shop would be done with this sublime idea behind it: I do it as a part of the world's work, and this is the duty that falls to my lot to do. It would be taken as coming directly from the great Will by which the worlds move, as your share of the Divine Activity, your part of the universal work; and the mightiest archangel, the greatest of the shining ones, can do nothing more than his share of carrying out the Divine Will. George Herbert (English poet and clergyman, 1593–1633) wrote truth when he said that the one who sweeps a room as to the glory of God makes that and the action fine. That is spiritual life, where all is done for duty, for the larger instead of for the smaller self.

It is not always easy. No shuffling, no leaving of a task undone because the Master's eye will not be there, for our Master's eye is everywhere, and he is never sleeping. No scamping of work, for that is not to be done by one of the

Divine Artificers, but only by an ignorant and clumsy worker. Art is only doing what you do perfectly, and God is always an artist. There is nothing, however small, no animal seen only in the microscope that is not perfect in its beauty. The more closely you examine it, the more exquisite does it become. With minute diatoms that you can only see through the microscope, every minute shell is sculptured with patterns geometrically perfect—for whom? For the satisfaction of that sense of perfection, which is one of the divine elements in God and humans alike. Not what you do, but how you do it, so that it is perfectly wrought to the utmost limit of your ability—that is the test of a person's character, and by the work you can know the character of the worker.

Now, that seems a small thing when you bring it down to your own house, shop, or office. Taken one by one, these things seem small, but suppose everyone did them. How would the face of the world then appear? No scamped work; no unreliable products on the market; nothing adulterated; nothing that was not what it pretended to be; the face value and the real value always identical; every house perfectly built; every drain perfectly laid; everything done as well as one's skill and strength can do it. Why, a world like that seems a fairy tale, an impossible Utopia, but that would be the result if all individuals did their duty as perfectly as their powers permitted. That is the first step towards the spiritual life. It is not outside your reach; it is close to everyone.

Self-Sacrifice

But that is not all; there is a higher stage of the spiritual life. It is much to feel yourself a coworker with the Divine in the world, much to make your work great by knitting it to the universal work throughout this mighty system of worlds and universes, much, too, as Emerson said, to hitch your wagon to a star, instead of to some miserable post by the wayside. But even that is not the most splendid thing you can attain. For there is one thing greater even than duty, and that is when all action is done as sacrifice.

Now, what does that mean? There would be no world, no

you, no I, if there had not been a primary sacrifice by which a fragment of the Divine Thought sheathed itself in matter, limited itself in order that you and I might become self-consciously divine. There is a profound truth in that great Christian teaching of a lamb slain—when? On Calvary? No, "from the foundation of the world." That is the great truth of sacrifice. No divine sacrifice, no universe. No divine self-limitations, none of the worlds which fill the realms of space. It is all a sacrifice, the sacrifice of love that limits itself so that others may gain self-conscious being and rejoice in the perfection of their own ultimate divinity. Inasmuch as the life of the world is based on sacrifice, all true life is also sacrificial; and when every action is done as sacrifice, then one becomes the perfect, spiritual person.

Now that is hard, although the first stage is not so difficult. We may make our lives useful; but how difficult it is—after our lives are wrapped up in some useful work—to be able to see that work shivered into pieces, and look on its ruins with calm content. That is one of the things that is meant by sacrifice. You may throw the whole of your life into some good work, the whole of your energy into some great scheme; you may toil and build and plan and shape; and you may nourish your own begotten scheme as a mother would cherish the child of her womb. Then presently it falls to pieces round you. It fails; it does not grow; it dies. Can you be content with such a result? After years of labor, years of thought, years of sacrifice, can you see everything crumble into dust and nothing remain? If not, then you are working for self and not as part of the Divine Activity. However gilded over with love of others your scheme may have been, it was your work and not God's work, and therefore you have suffered in the breaking. For if it were really his and not yours, if it were a sacrifice and not your own possession, you would know that all that is good in it must inevitably go into the forces of good in the world; that if he did not want the form you built, you would rather it were broken, and the life that cannot die go into other forms which fit better with the Divine Plan and work into the great scheme of evolution.

Let me put it another way, and you will see exactly what I mean, perhaps less abstractly. Take an army awaiting attack from some enemy greater and stronger than itself. The commander-in-chief maps out his scheme of battle, places one regiment in one spot and one regiment in another, makes one great plan that includes the whole. Then the day of battle dawns. From the side of the general goes a galloping messenger to send word to some young captain in one part of the field, "Go attack that fort that lies in front of you, capture it, and hold it until word comes to leave." The young captain, with his little band of young men behind him, looks at the fort in front, and knows he cannot take it, sees that failure is inevitable, knows that it means mutilation and death to the men under his command. He knows that if he carries out the order to the last, not one man of that little band may see tomorrow's sun, but every one will be swept away in the death-hail that will come upon them as they struggle up the hill to the impregnable fort at the top.

He sees it all. Does he hesitate? If he does he is a trator, dishonored, craven. He calls his men together. "Orders have come to take the fort!" They charge up at it and are decimated. Again they charge, and again they leave a tenth of their number on the slope. Again and again they charge, until no man is left there to stand and charge again.

Meanwhile, on another side of the field progress has been made with the general's plan; the attention of the enemy has been occupied by this handful of men who go cheerfully to death, and the plan has developed. For while the enemy watched the forlorn hope, the plan of their comrades was carried out on the other side. In the long run, when the sun sets, victory belongs to the army, although those men lie dead and dying on the slope.

Have they failed? It looks like failure to lie there dying and dead; surely the men have failed. But when the story of that battle is written, when a grateful nation raises a monument to the memory of the conquerors of that battle, high on that monument will be graven in imperishable gold the names of the men who died and made victory possible for their comrades by accepting defeat for themselves.

You read my parable. There is no failure where the commander-in-chief is the Divine Architect of the universe, no
failure, only inevitable success; and shall anyone who is
called to sacrifice not feel pride in order that the plan may
be carried out? There is no failure, for victory is ever on the
divine side. What does it matter if you and I look like fail-
ures; what does it matter if our petty plans crumble to pieces
in our hands; what does it matter if our schemes of a
moment are found to be useless and are thrown aside? The
life we have thrown into them, the devotion with which we
planned them, the strength with which we strove to carry
them out, the sacrifice with which we offered them to the
success of the mighty whole—these things enrolled us as
sacrificial workers with the Deity. No glory is greater than
the glory of the personal failure which ensures universal
success. That is only for the strong, granted, only for the
heroes. It is their work and their delight. But even to be able
to see the beauty in it is to bring some of the beauty into
every one of our lives. For seeing a thing as noble is to begin
to incarnate that nobility in your life. The mere recognition
of the splendor of an ideal is the first step towards becoming
transformed into its image.

Bringing the Divine Ideal into the World

Now suppose that you and I can shape our lives on lines
such as these which inadequately I have tried to sketch. We
shall become the spiritual person living in the world,
making the world slowly after the fashion of the Divine
Ideal, and making it more and more the perfectly manifested Divine Thought. That is the central idea, then, which
will transform the man or woman of the world into the
spiritual person, and in the world it can best be performed.
The life of the jungle is never the last life of a savior.
Sometimes such a life will be one of the many lives through
which he goes to gather universal experience—a time of
gathering strength and accumulating the power that is to be
used hereafter. But the life of the Christs of the race is the
life in the world, and not the life in the jungle. Though we
may sometimes profitably go into seclusion, the manifested

God walks in the haunts of men. For only there is the great work to be done, there the trials to be faced, there the powers to be opened up. When all our powers are brought out, when we are all of us Christs, then we can leave the outer life of the world to become part of its inner life, which shapes and molds the outer activity. But those who are only growing to that stature must grow by the law of growth, and that is the law of experience. Only the perfect may pass behind the veil and thence send out the spiritual powers unfolded in the life of the world.

It seems to be there is not one of us who may not begin to lead the truly spiritual life. The world will be the better for the living, while we will unfold the more rapidly for our effort. For all of us, if we only think of it, are at work to carve our own life into a perfect image, the image of the Divine manifest in humanity. It is not that the Divine is not within you; were it not so, how would you bring it forth? The ideal comes before the manifestation; the thought creates the form; and in every one of you there is sleeping, as it were, the divine image. Your work is to make that image manifest. Then you are the spiritual man or woman.

Come with me to the studio of some great sculptor, not a mere marble-chipper, but one of those geniuses who show the marble living and the ideal in spotless form. How does that person work? Do you think he is carving a statue out of the marble? He is doing nothing of the kind. He is setting free a statue within the marble, and cutting away the super-incumbent, useless marble that hides the beauty of the ideal that he sees. That is the sculptor of genius. In the rough block, which is all that you and I can see with our poor eyes, he sees the perfect statue imprisoned within the stone, and with every blow of mallet, with every deft touch of chisel, he brings that prisoner nearer to freedom, his ideal nearer to manifestation.

So it is with you and me: we are rough blocks of marble as we live here in the studio of the world, many of us, rough and unhewn, and the divinity within us hidden, as the statue within the block. You and I are sculptors, and by our life that statue is to be made manifest, that imprisoned beauty is to be set free. With the mallet of will, the chisel of thought, we must cut away all this superincumbent, useless stone that hides the living divinity within us, hides its unmanifested glory. Sculptors every one of you, shaping out what you shall inevitably be in years, in centuries, to come. The more skill, the more knowledge, the stronger will you have, the more powerfully you can use your mallet and your chisel, the swifter will come the day of liberation, the nearer the manifestation of the work.

Wherever you may be, in whatever workshop of this great world you may find yourself at labor, keep ever in your heart the ideal that you would realize. Feel the presence of the imprisoned divinity that you alone have the mighty privilege of liberating. Take in hand your tools, cut away the worthless stone, liberate the splendid statue. Then you shall know yourself self-consciously as that which you really are, a man or woman in the image of God.

2

Some Difficulties of the Inner Life

All those who set themselves in earnest to live the Inner Life encounter certain obstacles at the very beginning of the pathway. These obstacles repeat themselves in the experience of each person, having their basis in human nature. They seem new and peculiar to each wayfarer and give rise to a feeling of personal discouragement which undermines the strength needed to surmount them. If the neophyte understood that these obstacles form part of the common experience of aspirants, that they are always encountered and constantly overcome, the knowledge might bring some cheer. The grasp of a hand in the darkness, the sound of a voice that says, "Fellow-traveler, I have trodden where you tread and the road is practicable"—these things bring help, as I hope this article will.

One of these difficulties was put to me some time ago by a friend and fellow-wayfarer in connection with some counsel given as to the purification of the body. He said, with much truth and insight, that for most of us the difficulty lies more with us than with our instruments. For most of us our bodies are quite sufficiently good, or, at the worst, need a little tuning, but that there is a desperate need for improving the person within. For the lack of sweet music, the musicians are more to blame than their instruments, and if they could improve themselves their instruments might pass muster. The instruments are capable of yielding much better tones than they produce at present, but those tones depend on the fingers that press the keys. My friend said pithily and somewhat pathetically, "I can make my body do what I want; the difficulty is that *I* do not want."

Here is a difficulty that every serious aspirant feels. Improving ourselves is the chief thing that is needed, and the obstacle of our weakness, our lack of will and tenacity of purpose, is a far more obstructive one than can be placed in our way by the body. There are many methods known to all of us by which we can build up bodies of a better type if we want to do so, but it is the "wanting" in which we are deficient. We have the knowledge, we recognize the expediency of putting these methods into practice, but the impulse to do so is lacking. Our root-difficulty lies in our inner nature; it is inert, the wish to move is absent. It is not that the external obstacles are insurmountable, but that the one within lies supine and has no mind to climb over them.

We continually repeat this experience. There seems to be a want of attractiveness in our ideal; it fails to draw us. We do not wish to realize it, even though we may have intellectually decided that its realization is desirable. Our ideal stands before us like food before a person who is not hungry; it is certainly very good food and we may be glad of it tomorrow, but just now we have no craving for it and prefer to lie basking in the sunshine rather than to get up and take possession of it.

The problem resolves itself into two questions: Why do I not want that which I as a rational being see is desirable and productive of happiness? What can I do to make myself want that which I know to be best for myself and for the world? The spiritual teacher who could answer these questions effectively would do a far greater service to many than one who is only reiterating constantly the abstract desirability of ideals that we all acknowledge, and the imperative nature of obligations that we all admit—and disregard. The machine is here, not wholly ill-made; who can place a finger on the lever, *and make it go?*

Consciousness and Its Vehicles

The first question must be answered by such an analysis of self-consciousness as may explain this puzzling duality, the not desiring that which we see to be desirable. We say that self-consciousness is a unit, and yet, when we turn our attention inwards, we see a bewildering multiplicity of "I's," and are stunned by the clamor of opposing voices, all coming apparently from ourselves.

Now consciousness—and self-consciousness is only consciousness drawn into a definite center which receives and sends out—is a unit. If it appears in the outer world as many, this is not because consciousness has lost its unity, but because it presents itself there through different media. We speak glibly of the vehicles of consciousness, but perhaps do not always bear in mind what is implied in the phrase. If a current from a galvanic battery is led through a series of several different materials, its appearance will vary with each wire. In platinum it may appear as light, in iron as heat, around a bar of soft iron as magnetic energy, in a solution as a power that decomposes and recombines. One single energy is present, yet many modes of it appear, for the manifestation of life is always conditioned by its forms.

In like manner as consciousness works in the causal, mental, astral or physical body, the resulting "I" presents very different characteristics. According to the vehicle which, for the time being, it is vitalizing, so will be the conscious "I." If it is working in the astral body it will be the "I" of the senses; if in the mental, it will be the "I" of the intellect. By illusion, blinded by the material that enwraps it, it identifies itself with the craving of the senses, the reasoning of the intellect, and cries, "I want," "I think." The nature which is developing the germs of bliss and knowledge is the eternal Self within, and this is the root of sensations and thoughts.

These sensations and thoughts themselves are only the transitory activities in the outer bodies, set up by the contact of the inner life with the outer life, of the Self with the not-Self. The Self makes temporary centers for its life in one or other of these bodies, lured by the touches from without that awaken its activity, and working in these it identifies with them. As its evolution proceeds, as the Self develops, it gradually discovers that these physical, astral, mental centers are its instruments, not itself; it sees them as parts of the "not-Self" that it has temporarily attracted into union with it—as one might take up a pen or a chisel. The Self draws away from them, recognizing and using them as the tools they are. The Self knows itself to be life, not form, bliss, not desire, knowledge, not thought. Such a person is first conscious of unity, then alone finds peace. While the consciousness identifies itself with forms, it appears to be multiple; when it identifies itself as life, it stands forth as one.

The Place of Sensation, the Mind, and the Will

The next important fact for us is that, as H. P. Blavatsky, author of *The Secret Doctrine*, pointed out, consciousness at the present stage of evolution has its center normally in the astral body. Consciousness learns to know by its capacity for sensation, the sensation which belongs to the astral body. We sense; that is, we recognize contact with something which is not ourselves, something which arouses in us pleasure or pain, or the neutral point between.

This life of sensation is the greater part of the life of the majority. For those below the average, this life of sensation is the whole life. For a few advanced beings this life of sensation is transcended. The vast majority occupy the various stages which stretch between the life of sensation and that which has transcended such sensation: stages of mixed sensation, emotion and thought in diverse proportions.

In the life wholly of sensation there is no multiplicity of "I's," and therefore no conflict; in the life that has transcended sensation there is an Inner Ruler Immortal, and there is no conflict. But in all the ranges between there are manifold "I's" and among them conflict.

Let us consider this life of sensation as found in those whose development lies there. There is an "I," passionate, craving, fierce, grasping, when aroused to activity. But there is no conflict, except with the world outside the physical body. With that such people may war, but they do not know inner strife. They do what they want, without questionings beforehand or remorse afterwards. The actions of the body follow the promptings of desire, and the mind does not challenge, nor criticize, nor condemn. It merely pictures and records, storing up materials for future elaboration. Its evolution is forwarded by the demands made upon it by the "I" of sensations to exert its energies for the gratification of that imperious "I."

Awakening of the Mind

The mind is driven into activity by these promptings of desire and begins to work on its store of observations and remembrances, thus evolving a little reasoning faculty and planning beforehand for the gratification of that "I." In this way it develops intelligence, but the intelligence is wholly subordinated to desire, moves under its orders, and is the slave of passion. It shows no separate individuality, but is merely the willing tool of the tyrannous desire-"I."

Contest begins only when, after a long series of experiences, the Eternal Self has developed sufficient mind to review and balance up, during its life in the lower mental world between death and birth, the results of its earthly activities. It then marks off certain experiences as resulting in more pain than pleasure, and comes to the conclusion that it will do well to avoid their repetition; it regards them with repulsion and engraves that repulsion on its mental tablets, while similarly engraving attraction as regards other experiences that have resulted in more pleasure than pain. When the Eternal Self returns to earth, it brings this record along as an inner tendency of mind. When the desire-"I" rushes towards an attractive object, recommencing a course of experiences that have led to suffering, it interposes a feeble protest. Another "I"—consciousness working as mind—makes itself felt and heard as regarding these experiences with repulsion and objecting to being dragged through them.

The protest is so weak and the desire so strong that we can scarcely speak of a contest; the desire-"I," long enthroned, rushes over the weakly protesting rebel. But when the pleasure is over and the painful results follow, the ignored rebel lifts its voice again in a querulous "I told you so," and this is the first sting of remorse.

As life succeeds life, the mind asserts itself more and more, and the contest between the desire-"I" and the thought-"I" grows more and more fierce. The agonized cry of the Christian mystic, "I find another law in my members warring against the law of my mind," is repeated in the experience of every evolving Self. The war grows hotter and hotter as, during the devachanic life, the decisions of the inner Self are more and more strongly impressed on the mind, appearing as innate ideas in the subsequent birth, and lending strength to the thought-"I." Thus "I," withdrawing itself from the passions and emotions, regards these as outside itself and repudiates their claim to control it. But the long inheritance of the past is on the side of the monarch it would discrown, and the war is bitter and many-fortuned. Consciousness, in its outgoing activities, runs easily into the worn channels of the habits of many lives. On the other hand, it is diverted by the efforts of the Self to take control and turn it into the channels hewn out by its own reflections.

The inner will determines the line of the consciousness-forces working in the higher vehicles, while habit largely determines the direction of those working in the desire body. The will, guided by the clear-eyed intelligence, points to the lofty ideal that is seen as a fit object of attainment. The desire-nature does not want to reach it, is lethargic before it, not seeing its beauty, often repelled by the austere outlines of its grave and chastened dignity. "The difficulty is that I do not *want*." We do not want to do that which, in our higher moments, we have resolved to do. The lower "I" is moved by the attraction of the moment rather than by the recorded results of the past that sway the higher "I." The real difficulty is to make ourselves feel that the lethargic or clamorous "I" of the lower nature is not the true "I."

How is this difficulty to be overcome? How is it possible to make that which we know to be the higher to be the habitual self-conscious "I"?

Let no one be discouraged that this change is a matter of growth and cannot be accomplished in a moment. The human Self cannot, by a single effort, rise to adulthood from childhood, any more than a body can change from infancy to maturity in a night. If the statement of the law of growth brings a sense of chill when we regard it as an obstacle in the way of our wish for sudden perfection, let us remember the other side of the statement: growth is certain; it cannot be ultimately prevented. If law refuses a miracle, on the other hand, it gives security. Moreover, we can quicken growth. We can provide the best possible conditions for it, and then rely on the law for our result.

Let us then consider the means we can employ for hastening the growth we see to be needed, for transferring the activity of consciousness from the lower to the higher.

The first thing to realize is that the desire-nature is not our Self but an instrument fashioned by the Self for its own use; and next, that it is a most valuable instrument, and is merely being badly used. Desire or emotion is the motive power in us and stands ever between thought and action. Intellect sees, but it does not move. A person without desires and emotions would be a mere spectator of life. The Self must have evolved some of its loftiest powers before it can forgo the use of the desires and emotions; for aspirants the question is how to use them instead of being used by them, how to discipline them, not how to destroy them. We would "want" to reach the highest, since without this wanting we shall make no progress at all. We are held back by wanting to unite ourselves with transitory, mean and narrow objects. Cannot we push ourselves forward by wanting to unite ourselves with the permanent, the noble and the wide?

Ennobling the Emotions

Thus musing, we see that what we need is to cultivate the emotions and direct them in a way that will purify and ennoble the character. The basis of all emotions on the side of progress is love, and this is the power we must cultivate.

Novelist George Eliot well said, "The first condition of human goodness is something to love; the second, something to reverence."

Now reverence is only love directed to a superior, and aspirants should seek one more advanced than themselves to whom they can direct love and reverence. Finding one to revere gives aspirants the most important condition for turning emotion from a retarding force into a lifting one, and for gaining the needed power to "want" that which they know to be the best. We cannot love without seeking to please, and we cannot reverence without taking joy in the approval of the one we revere. Hence comes a constant stimulus to improve ourselves, to build up character, to purify our nature, to conquer all in us that is base, to strive after all that is worthy. We find ourselves quite spontaneously "wanting" to reach a high ideal, and the great motive power is sent along the channels hewn out for it by the mind. There is no way of utilizing the desire-nature more certain and more effective than making such a tie, the reflection in the lower world of that perfect bond which links the disciple to the Master.

Another useful way of stimulating the desire-nature as a lifting force is to seek the company of any who are more advanced in the spiritual life than we are ourselves. It is not necessary that they should teach us orally, nor indeed talk to us at all. Their very presence is a benediction, harmonizing, raising, inspiring. To breathe their atmosphere, to be encircled by their magnetism, to be played on by their thoughts—these things ennoble us, unconsciously to ourselves. We value words too highly and depreciate unduly the subtler silent forces of the Self, which, "sweetly and mightily ordering all things," create within the turbulent chaos of our personality the sure bases of peace and truth.

Less potent, but still sure, is the help that may be gained by reading any book which strikes a noble note, whether by holding up a great ideal or by presenting an inspiring character for our study. Such books as the *Bhagavad-Gita, The Voice of the Silence, Light on the Path, The Imitation of Christ* are among the most powerful of such aids to the desire-nature. We are apt to read too exclusively for knowledge, and lose the molding force that lofty thought on great ideals may exercise over our emotions. It is a useful habit to read a few sentences from some such book every morning and to carry these sentences with us through the day, thus creating around us an atmosphere that is protective to ourselves and beneficial to all with whom we come into contact.

Another absolutely essential thing is daily meditation—a quiet half-hour in the morning, before the turmoil of the day begins, during which we deliberately draw ourselves away from the lower nature, recognize it as an instrument and not our Self, center ourselves in the highest consciousness we can dream, and feel it as our real Self. "That which is Being, Bliss and Knowledge, that am I. Life, Love and Light, that am I." For our essential nature is divine, and the effort to realize it helps its growth and manifestation. Pure, passionless, peaceful, it is "the Star that shines within," and that Star is our Self. We cannot yet steadily dwell in the Star, but as we try daily to rise to it, some gleam of its radiance illumines the illusory "I" made of the shadows amid which we live. We may fitly rise to this ennobling and peace-giving contemplation of our divine destiny by worshipping with the most fervent devotion of which we are capable—if we are fortunate enough to feel such devotion—the Father of the worlds and the Divine Being whom we reverence as Master. Resting on that Divine Being as the helper and lover of all who seek to rise—call him Buddha, Christ, Sri Krishna, Master, what we will—we may dare to raise our eyes to the One from whom we come, to whom we go, and in the confidence of realized sonship murmur, "I and the Father are One," "I am That."

The Ebb and Flow of Feelings

One of the most distressing difficulties aspirants have to face arises from the ebb and flow of their feelings, the changes in the emotional atmosphere through which they see the external world as well as their own character with its powers and its weaknesses. They find that their life consists

of a series of ever-varying states of consciousness, of alter-
nating conditions of thought and feeling. At one time they
are vividly alive, at another quiescently dead; now cheerful,
then morbid; now overflowing, then dry; now earnest, then
indifferent; now devoted, then cold; now aspiring, then
lethargic. They are constant only in this changeableness,
persistent only in this variety. And the worst of it is that they
are unable to trace these effects to definite causes; they
"come and go, impermanent," and are as little predictable
as the summer winds.

Why was meditation easy, smooth, fruitful, yesterday?
Why is it hard, irregular, barren, today? Why should that
noble idea have fired us with enthusiasm a week ago, yet
leave us chill now? Why were we full of love and devotion a
few days ago, but find ourselves empty now, gazing at our
ideal with cold, lack-luster eyes? The facts are obvious, but
the explanation escapes us; we seem to be at the mercy of
chance, to have slipped out of the realm of law.

It is this very uncertainty which gives the poignancy to
our distress. The understood is always the manageable, and
when we have traced an effect to its cause we have gone far
on the way to its control. All our keenest sufferings have in
them this constituent of uncertainty; we are helpless because we are ignorant. It is the uncertainty of our emotional
moods that terrifies us, for we cannot guard against that
which we are unable to foresee. How then may we reach a
place where these moods shall not plague us, a rock on
which we can stand while the waves surge around us?

The first step towards the place of balance is taken when
we recognize the fact—though the statement of it may
sound brutal—that our moods do not matter. There is no
constant relation between our progress and our feelings; we
are not necessarily advancing when the flow of emotion
makes us rejoice, nor retrograding when its ebb distresses
us. These changing moods are among the lessons that life
brings to us, that we may learn to distinguish between the
Self and the not-Self, and to realize ourselves as the Self.
The Self does not change; that which changes is not our Self,
but is part of the transitory surroundings in which the Self

is clothed and amid which it moves. This wave that sweeps over us is not the Self, but is only a passing manifestation of the not-Self. "Let it toss and swirl and foam; it is not I." Let consciousness realize this, if only for a moment, and the force of the wave is spent; and the firm rock is felt under our feet. Withdrawing from the emotion, we no longer feel it as a part of ourselves; thus ceasing to pour our life into it as self-expression, we break off the connection which enabled it to become a channel of pain. This withdrawal of consciousness may be much facilitated if, in our quiet times, we try to understand these distressing emotional alternations and assign them to their true causes. We shall thus at least get rid of some of the helplessness and perplexity which, as we have already seen, are due to ignorance.

These alternations of happiness and depression are primarily manifestations of that law of periodicity, or law of rhythm, which guides the universe. Night and day alternate in our physical life as do happiness and depression in our emotional life. As the ebb and flow of the ocean, so are the ebb and flow in human feelings. There are tides in the human heart and in human affairs as in the sea. Joy follows sorrow and sorrow follows joy, as surely as death follows birth and birth death. That this is so is not only a theory; it is a fact borne witness to by all who have gained experience in the spiritual life. In Thomas à Kempis's *Imitation of Christ*, it is said that comfort and sorrow thus alternate, and "this is nothing new nor strange unto them that have experience in the way of God; for the great saints and ancient prophets had oftentimes experience of such kind of vicissitudes. . . . If great saints were so dealt with, we that are weak and poor ought not to despair if we be sometimes hot and sometimes cold. . . . I never found any so religious and devout, that he had not sometimes a withdrawing of grace or felt not some decrease of zeal" (Bk. II, ix, 4, 5, 7).

Recognizing this alternation of states as the result of a general law, a special manifestation of a universal principle, it becomes possible for us to utilize this knowledge both as a warning and an encouragement. We may be passing through a period of great spiritual illumination when all seems easy to accomplish, when the glow of devotion sheds its glory over life, and when the peace of sure insight is ours. Such a condition is often one of considerable danger, its very happiness lulling us into a careless security and forcing into growth any remaining germs of the lower nature. At such moments recalling past periods of gloom is often useful, so that happiness may not become elation, nor enjoyment lead to attachment to pleasure. Balancing the present joy by the memory of past trouble and the calm prevision of trouble yet to come, we reach equilibrium and find a middle point of rest.

We can then gain all the advantages that accrue from seizing a favorable opportunity for progress without risking a slip backwards from premature triumph. When the night comes down and all the life has ebbed away, when we find ourselves cold and indifferent, caring for nothing that had attracted us, then, knowing the law, we can quietly say, "This also will pass in its turn; light and life must come back, and the old love will again glow warmly." We refuse to be unduly depressed in the gloom, as we refused to be unduly elated in the light. We balance one experience against the other, removing the thorn of present pain by the memory of past joy and the foretaste of joy in the future. We learn in happiness to remember sorrow and in sorrow to remember happiness, till neither one nor the other can shake the steady foothold of the soul.

Thus we begin to rise above the lower stages of consciousness in which we are flung from one extreme to the other, and to gain the equilibrium which is called yoga. Thus the existence of the law becomes to us not a theory but a conviction, and we gradually learn something of the peace of the Self.

Tests and Trials

It may be well also for us to realize that the way in which we face and live through this trial of inner darkness and deadness is one of the surest tests of spiritual evolution. "What worldly man is there that would not willingly receive spiritual joy and comfort if he could always have it?

For spiritual comforts exceed all the delights of the world and the pleasures of the flesh. . . . But no man can always enjoy these divine comforts according to his desire; for the time of trial is never far away. . . . Are not all those to be called mercenary who are ever seeking consolations? . . . Where shall one be found who is willing to serve God for nought? Rarely is anyone found so spiritual as to have suffered the loss of all things" (*Imitation of Christ*, Bk. II. x. 1; xi. 3, 4).

The subtle germs of selfishness persist far on into the life of discipleship, though they then ape in their growth of the semblance of virtues and hide the serpent of desire under the fair blossom of beneficence or of devotion. Few indeed are they who serve for nothing, who have eradicated the root of desire and not merely cut off the branches that spread above ground. Many who have tasted the subtle joys of spiritual experience find therein reward for the grosser delights they have renounced. When the keen ordeal of spiritual darkness bars their way, and they have to enter into that darkness unbefriended and apparently alone, then they learn by the bitter and humiliating lesson of disillusion that they have been serving their ideal for wages and not for love. It is well for us if we can be glad in the darkness as well as in the light, by the sure faith in—though not yet by the vision of— that Flame which burns ever within, That from the light of which we can never be separated, for it is in truth our very Self. We must be bankrupt in Time before the wealth of the eternal is ours.

Another difficulty that sorely bewilders and distresses aspirants is the unbidden presence of thoughts and desires that are incongruous with their life and aims. When they would contemplate the holy, the presence of the unholy thrusts itself upon them; when they would see the radiant face of the Divine One, the mask of the satyr leers in its stead. Where do these thronging forms of evil that crowd around come from? Whence these mutterings and whisperings as of devils in one's ear? They fill aspirants with shuddering repulsion, yet seem to be their own. Can an aspirant really be the parent of this foul swarm?

Once again an understanding of the cause at work may rob the effect of its sharp poison-tooth, and deliver us from impotence due to ignorance.

It is a commonplace of theosophical teaching that life embodies itself in forms, and the life-energy which comes forth from that aspect of the Self which is knowledge molds the matter of the mental plane into thought-forms. The vibrations that affect the mental body determine the materials that are built into its composition, and these materials are slowly changed in accordance with the changes in the vibrations sent forth. If the consciousness ceases to work in a particular way, the materials which answered to those previous workings gradually lose their activity, finally becoming effete matter and being shaken out of the mental body. A considerable number of stages, however, intervene between the full activity of the matter constantly answering to mental impulses and its final deadness when ready for expulsion. Until the last stage is reached, the mental matter is capable of being thrown into renewed activity by mental impulses, either from within or from without. Long after the person has ceased to energize it, having outgrown the stage it represents, it may be thrown into active vibration and made to start up as a living thought by a wholly external influence.

For example, we have succeeded in purifying our thoughts from sensuality, and our mind no longer generates impure ideas nor takes pleasure in contemplating impure images. We are no longer vivifying the coarse matter, which in the mental and astral bodies vibrates under such impulses, and the thought-forms we created are dying or dead. But we meet someone in whom these things are active, and the vibrations sent out by that person revivify the dying thought-forms, lending them a temporary artificial life. They appear as our own thoughts, presenting themselves as the children of our mind, and we do not know that they are but corpses from our past, reanimated by the evil magic of impure propinquity. The very contrast they afford to our purified mind adds to the harassing torture of their presence, as though a dead body were fettered to a living person. But when we learn their true nature, they lose their power to torment. We can look at them calmly as remnants of our past, so that they cease to poison our present. We know that the life in them is an alien one and is not drawn from us and we can "wait with the patience of confidence for the hour when they shall affect us no longer."

Sometimes in the case of a person who is making rapid progress, this temporary revivification is caused deliberately by those who are seeking to retard evolution, those who set themselves against the Good Law. They may send a thought-force calculated to stir the dying ghosts into weird activity, with the set purpose of causing distress, even when the aspirant has passed beyond the reach of temptation along these lines. Once again, the difficulty ceases when the thoughts are known to draw their energy from outside and not from inside, when one can calmly say to the surging crowd of impish tormentors: "You are not mine, you are no part of me, your life is not drawn from my thought. Before long you will be dead beyond possibility of resurrection, and meanwhile you are but phantoms, shades that were once my foes."

Another fruitful source of trouble is the great magician Time, past-master of illusion. Time imposes on us a sense of hurry, of unrest, by masking the oneness of our life with the veils of births and deaths. The aspirant cries out eagerly, "How much can I do, what progress can I make, during my present life?" There is no such thing as a "present life"; there is but one life—past and future, with the ever-changing moment that is their meetingplace. On one side of it we see the past and on the other side the future; and it is itself as invisible as the little piece of ground on which we stand. There is but one life, without beginning and without end-ing, the ageless, timeless life, and our arbitrary divisions of it by the ever-recurring incidents of births and deaths delude and ensnare us. These are some of the traps set for the Self by the lower nature, which would keep its hold on the winged immortal that is straying through its miry paths. This bird of paradise is so fair a thing, as its plumes begin to grow, that all the powers of nature fall to loving it. They set snares to hold it prisoner; and of all the snares the illusion of Time is the most subtle.

When a vision of truth has come late in one's physical life, this discouragement as to time is apt to be most keenly felt. "I am too old to begin; if I had only known this in youth," is the cry. Yet truly the path is one, as the life is one, and all the path must be trodden in the life. What does it matter then whether one stage of the path is trodden during a particular part of a physical life? If A and B are both going to catch their first glimpse of the Reality two years hence, what does it matter that A will then be seventy years of age while B will be a youth of twenty? A will return and begin work on earth anew when B is ageing. Each will pass many times through the childhood, youth and old age of the body, while traveling along the higher stages of the path of life. The old person who "late in life," as we say, begins to learn the truths of the Ancient Wisdom, instead of lamenting over his age and saying "How little can I do in the short time that remains to me," should say, "How good a foundation I can lay for my next incarnation, thanks to learning the truth."

We are not slaves of Time, unless we bow to his imperious tyranny and let him bind our eyes with the bandages of birth and death. We are always ourselves, and can pace steadfastly onwards through the changing lights and shadows cast by Time's magic lantern on the life he cannot age. Why are the gods figured as ever-young, except to remind us that the true life lives untouched by Time? We borrow some of the strength and calm of Eternity when we try to live in it, escaping from the meshes of the great Enchanter.

Many other difficulties will stretch across the upward path as the aspirant treads it. A resolute will and a devoted heart, lighted by knowledge, will conquer all in the end and will bring everyone to the supreme goal. To rest on the Law is one of the secrets of peace, to trust it utterly at all times, especially when the gloom descends. No soul that aspires can ever fail to rise; no heart that loves can ever be abandoned. Difficulties exist only that in overcoming them we may grow strong, and only those who have suffered are able to save.

3

The Place of Peace

Everyone complains about the rush, the turmoil, the hurry of modern life. "I have no time" is the commonest excuse. Reviews substitute for books, leading articles for political treatises, lectures for investigation. More and more our attention is fastened on the superficial things of life: small prizes of business success, petty prestige of social supremacy, momentary notoriety in the world of politics or letters—men and women toil, intrigue and strive for these things.

Our work must show immediate results or it is regarded as failure; the goal post must always be in sight, to be passed by a swift, brief effort, with the roar of the applauding crowd hailing the winner. The solid reputation built up by years of strenuous work; the patient toil of a lifetime in a field which the harvest can ripen only long after the sower has passed out of sight; the deliberate choice of a lofty ideal, too high to attract the average person, too great to be compassed in a lifetime—all these things are passed by with a shrug of good-natured contempt or a scowl of suspicion. The spirit of the age is summed up by the words of the caustic Chinese sage, "He looks at an egg, and expects to hear it crow." Nature is too slow for us, and we forget that what we gain in speed we lose in depth.

But there are some in whose eyes this whirling dance of gnats in the sunlight is not the be-all and end-all of human life. In some hearts a whisper sometimes sounds softly, saying that all the seeming clash and rush is but the struggle of shadows thrown upon a screen; that social success, business

31

triumph, public admiration are trivial things at best, bubbles floating down a tossing stream, unworthy of the rivalries, the jealousies, the bitternesses their chase engenders. Has life no secret that does not lie on the surface, no problem that is not solved in the stating, no treasury that is not scattered on the highway?

Soothed by Nature

An answer may be found without straying beyond the experience of every man and woman, an answer that hides within it a suggestion of a deeper underlying truth. Suppose we spend a week or a month in hurried city life, with small excitements, striving for the little triumphs of social life, the eagerness of petty hopes, the pain of petty disappointments, the friction from our selfish selves jarring with other selves equally selfish. After this, suppose we go away from this hum and buzz into silent mountain solitudes. There we hear only natural harmonies that seem to blend with rather than break the silence—the rushing of the waterfall swollen by last night's rain, the rustle of the leaves under the timid feet of the hare, the whisper of the stream to the water hen as she slips out of the reeds, the murmur of the eddy lapping against the pebbles on the bank, the hum of insects brushing through the tangle of the grasses, the suck of fish as they hang in the pool beneath the shade. There, where the mind sinks into a calm, soothed by the touch of Nature far from human life, how important are the follies, the exasperations, of the social whirl of work and play? Seen through that atmosphere surcharged with peace, what does it matter if we failed or we succeeded in some small strife? What does it matter that we were slighted by one person, praised by another? We regain perspective by our distance from the whirlpool, by isolation from its tossing waters, and we see how small a part these outer things should play in our true life.

Time's Healing

Distance in time as well as distance in space gives balanced judgment on life. After ten years have slipped away, we look back at the trials, the joys, the hopes, the disappointments of that earlier time and we marvel that we spent so much of our energy on things of so little worth. Even life's sharpest pains seem strangely unreal when contemplated by a personality that has greatly changed. Our whole life was bound up in the life of another, and any value it held for us seemed to dwell in that beloved one. We thought that our life was over, our heart broken, when that one betrayed our trust. But as time went on the wound healed. Today we look back without a quiver on an agony that nearly shattered our life. Or we broke with a friend for a bitter word; how foolish our anger and excitement seem, looking back after ten years. Or we were elated by a hard-won success; how trivial it looks and how exaggerated our triumph, when we see it in due proportion in the picture of our life; then it filled our sky, now it is but a point.

This philosophic calm, as we contemplate the victories and defeats of our past across the interval of space or time, suffers an ignominious breach when we return to our daily life. All the old trivialities, in new dress, engross us; old joys and sorrows, with new faces, seize us. As the *Bhagavad Gita* says, "The tumultuous senses and organs hurry away by force the heart." Again we begin to wear out our lives by petty cares, petty disputes, petty longings, petty disappointments.

Must this be always so? Since we must live in the world and play our part in its drama, must we be at the mercy of these passing objects? Or, though we must dwell among them in space and be surrounded with them in time, can we find the Place of Peace, as though we were far away? We can, and this is the truth that underlies the superficial answer we have already found.

The Peace of the True Self

We are each an Immortal Being in a garb of flesh, which is vivified and moved by desires and passions. We link this garb to ourselves by a thread of our immortal nature. This thread is the mind, and this mind, unsubdued and inconstant, wanders out among the things of earth. It is moved by passions and desires, hopes and fears. It longs to taste all cups of sense-delights and is dazzled and deafened by the radiance and tumult of its surroundings. And thus, as Arjuna complained in the *Bhagavad Gita*, the "mind is full of agitation, turbulent, strong and obstinate."

Above this whirling mind as serene and passionless witness dwells the True Self, the Spiritual Ego. Below there may be storms, but above there is calm, the Place of Peace. For that Self is eternal. Of what importance are the things of time to it, except as they bring experience and the knowledge of good and evil? So often, dwelling in its house of clay, it has known birth and death, gains and losses, joys and griefs, pleasures and pains. It sees them all pass as a moving phantasmagoria, and no ripple ruffles its passionless serenity. If agony does affect its outer case, it merely notices that harmony has been broken. The pain is welcome as pointing to a failure and as bearing the lesson to avoid that from which it sprang. For the True Self has to conquer the material plane, to purify and sublimate it, and only by suffering can it learn how to perform its work.

Now the secret of reaching that Place of Peace lies in our learning to identify our consciousness with the True Self instead of with the apparent one. We identify ourselves with our minds, our brain minds, active in our bodies. We identify ourselves with our passions and desires and say *we* hope or *we* fear. We identify ourselves with our bodies, the mere machinery with which we affect the material world. When all these parts of our nature are moved by contact with external things and feel the whirl of the material life around them, *we* also in consciousness are affected. According to the *Gita*, "the uncontrolled heart, following the dictates of the moving passions, snatcheth away" our "spiritual knowledge, as the storm the bark upon the raging ocean." This results in excitement, loss of balance, irritability, injured feelings, resentments, follies, pain—all that is most separated from peace and calm and strength.

Three Ways to Peace

The way to begin to tread the Path that leads to the Place of Peace is to endeavor to identify our consciousness with the

True Self, to see as it sees, to judge as it judges. We cannot do it—that goes without saying—but we can begin to try. The means are: Disengaging from the objects of the senses, not caring about results, and meditation, ever renewed, on the True Self. Let us consider each of these means.

We can gain the first of these only by a constant and wise self-discipline. We can cultivate indifference to small discomforts, to pleasures of the table, to physical enjoyments, bearing outward things with good-humored tolerance as they come, neither shunning nor courting small pleasures and pains. Gradually, without growing morbid or self-conscious, we become indifferent, so that small troubles that upset most people continually in daily life pass unnoticed. This will leave us free to help our neighbors, whom such troubles do disturb, by shielding them unobtrusively, and so smoothing life's pathway for feet tenderer than our own. In learning this, moderation is the keynote. "This divine discipline, Arjuna, is not to be attained by the man who eateth more than enough or too little, nor by him who hath a habit of sleeping much, nor by him who is given to overwatching. The meditation which destroyeth pain is produced in him who is moderate in eating and in recreation, of moderate exertion in his actions, and regulated in sleeping and waking." The body is not to be shattered: it is to be trained.

The second of these methods is not caring for results. This does not mean that we do not notice the result of our actions in order to learn from them how to guide our steps. We gain experience by such study of results, and so learn wisdom. It does mean that when an action has been done with our best judgment and strength and with pure intent, then we should let it go, metaphorically, and feel no anxiety about its results. The action done is beyond recall, and we gain nothing by worry and anxiety over it. When its results appear, we note them for instruction, but we neither rejoice nor mourn over them. Remorse or jubilation takes our attention away from performance of our *present* duty, and weakens us in that. Suppose the results of something we did are harmful. The wise person says, "I made a mistake and must avoid a similar blunder in future; but remorse will only weaken my present usefulness and will not lessen the results of my mistaken action. So instead of wasting time in remorse, I will set to work to do better."

The value of thus separating oneself from results lies in the calmness of mind obtained and the concentration brought to bear on each action. Says the Gita, "Whoever in acting dedicates his actions to the Supreme Spirit [the One Self] and puts aside all selfish interest in their result, is untouched by sin, even as the leaf of the lotus is unaffected by the waters. The truly devoted, for the purification of the heart, perform actions with their bodies, their minds, their understanding, and their senses, putting away all self-interest. The man who is devoted and not attached to the fruit of his actions obtains tranquility; whilst he who through desire has attachment for the fruit of action is bound down thereby."

The third method, meditation, is the most efficacious and the most difficult. It consists of a constant endeavor to realize our identity with our True Self, and to become self-conscious as It. "To whatsoever object the inconstant mind goeth out he should subdue it, bring it back, and place it upon the Spirit." It is a work of a lifetime, but it will bring us to the Place of Peace. We must continually renew the effort and patiently persist in it. This may be aided by setting aside a few moments, at a definite hour each day to withdraw ourselves like the turtle into its shell, and remember that we are not transitory but eternal and that passing incidents cannot affect us at all.

With the gradual growth of this power of remaining "in the Self" comes not only peace but wisdom, for absence of personal desires and recognition of our immortal nature leave us free to judge all things without bias or prejudice. "This tranquil state attained, therefrom shall soon result a separation from all troubles; and his mind being thus at ease, fixed upon one object, it embraceth wisdom from all sides. The man whose heart and mind are not at rest is without wisdom." Thus "being possessed of patience, he by degrees finds rest," and "supreme bliss surely cometh to the sage whose mind is thus at peace; whose passions and desires are thus subdued; who is thus in the True Self and free from sin."

This is the threefold Path that leads to the Place of Peace. To dwell there is to have conquered Time and Death. The "path winds uphill all the way," but the wings of the Dove of Peace fan the brow of the wearied pilgrim, and at last he finds the calm that nothing can ruffle.

4

Devotion and the Spiritual Life

> The soul cannot be gained by knowledge, nor by under-
> standing, nor by manifold science, . . . nor by devotion, nor
> by knowledge which is unwedded to devotion.
>
> (Mundakopanishad, iii. II. 3, 4)

According to the Upanishads, the oldest scripture of our
race, there are two paths for finding the Self. They may be
trodden separately, but must finally blend into one for the
perfection of humanity. One is the path of knowledge, and
it leads to liberation; the other is the path of devotion, and
that, joined to right knowledge, leads to that service which
is humanity's greatest glory to attain.

There are paths followed by those who have not yet taken
on the duty of discipleship, but who are good and earnest in
their lives and doing good work in the world. These are the
paths of action, paths where good action and good desire
generate good karma. But karma always bring one back to
rebirth. Myriads of years, in some cases millions of years,
may intervene, but the end of work is rebirth, the end of
desire is to "pass from death to deaths." Works that are good
and useful to humanity result in reward. Putting it in Christian terms, we should say that by them one gains Heaven; in
Hindu terms, one gains Svarga; in Theosophic parlance,
Devachan. Beyond the temporary Devachan or Svarga or
Heaven, there is a possibility of work done so well, with a
view always to its results, that one may reach that Heaven
of the cosmic Devas of which you read in Hindu writings.
Here one who has passed beyond ordinary humanity, and

by effort won these higher seats in Heaven, may reign throughout the course of a manvantara or cosmic period of manifestation, and direct the cosmic processes of the worlds.

But what comes from work finds its end. Neither Liberation nor the Great Renunciation can close the path of one who works with a view to results. For Nature is ever just; we will obtain what we pay for. If we work for the sake of reward, the reward will come from the unerring justice that guides the worlds. Good deeds become exhausted; the result of good karma comes to an end; and, whether in this or in any other world, the end is sure, and the Ego must come back to rebirth, as it has worked for reward and that reward at length is exhausted.

But, according to the scripture quoted above, there is a time when the worlds of works are exhausted. Then comes the time of which it is written:

> Let the Brahmin, after he has examined all these worlds that are gained by works, acquire freedom from all desire. Nothing that is eternal can be gained by what is not eternal.
>
> (Mundakopanishad, i. II. 12)

When all desire is exhausted then the path of knowledge or of devotion may be entered.

The Path of Knowledge

Let us take the path of knowledge. Knowledge of what? Not worldly learning; not those many sciences which may be gained by the intellect alone; nor even the mastery of the categories into which all human learning is divided. When we speak of the path of knowledge we mean more than intellectual learning. We mean the path which leads to spiritual knowledge, that is, to the knowledge of the One, of the Self, seeking and finding God or Brahman. For by knowledge the Divine may be found; by knowledge That may be entered into.

There are some who choose the path of knowledge unallied to devotion, and who tread that path life after life until they gain the right to liberation. Let us try to realize the steps of such a path.

First, there must be knowledge and recognition of the One on whom all worlds are built, the Self eternal and unchanging that throws out universes, as a spider throws out webs, and draws them in again (Mundakopanishad, i. I. 7). One must recognize the one Existence which is at the root of all, supreme, incognizable by human thought, the One without a second.

The next stage in that knowledge, in recognizing the One, is the realization that all things that take on separate forms must have an end, that there is no separateness in the universe, but only the appearance of separation. The One without a second who alone exists, who is the one Reality, *That* is realized as the Self of each, the One Life of which all forms are only transient manifestations. Until absence of separateness is realized the soul passes from death to death (Kathopanishad, Valli iv. 10).

But more than this realization of nonseparateness is needed. One must make a distinct and deliberate effort to realize that the Self of the universe is the Self dwelling in the human heart, that that Self becomes clothed in sheath after sheath for the purpose of gathering experience. On the path of knowledge sheath after sheath is stripped from the Self, until the very Self is found.

Knowledge is necessary for this: first the knowledge of the existence of the sheaths; then the knowledge of the Self working within the sheaths; then the realization that those sheaths can be laid aside one after another, that the senses can be stilled and silenced, that the Self can withdraw from the sheath of the senses until they no longer function except when one wills them to. Then the voice of the Self may be heard without the intrusion of the outer world.

Renunciation

The sheath of the mind in which the Self works in the internal world of concepts and ideas is also recognized as external to the Self, and the Self casts that aside as it casts off the sheath of the senses. Realizing that these sheaths are not itself, that the Self is behind and within them, this knowledge of nonseparateness becomes a practical realization, not only admitted intellectually, but realized practically in life. This must inevitably lead to renunciation. But it is the renunciation essentially of the reason, the renunciation which draws itself away from the objects of the senses and of the mind by deliberately retiring with the Self. This exclusion from the outer and inner worlds is most easily followed by retiring from human haunts, by the Self separating itself from all others that are illusory. In that external quietude the Self realizes the inner isolation.

If absolute exclusion of the outer and inner worlds is not accepted, there may still be renunciation by knowledge, by the deliberate will that no karma shall be generated, by the knowledge that if there is no desire, then no chains of karma are made to draw the Self back to rebirth. It is essentially the renunciation of those who know that while they desire they are bound to the wheel of births and deaths, and that no liberation is possible unless these bonds of the heart are broken. Then, realizing this, if these aspirants are still compelled to act, they will act without desire; if compelled to live among people, they will do their work not caring for the results that flow from it. Renunciation is complete, but for the sake of escape, to gain freedom and escape from the burden of the world. Again, it is written:

> When they have reached the Self [that is, when they have realized Brahman] the Sages become satisfied through knowledge; they are conscious of their Self, their passions have passed away and they are tranquil. The wise having reached Him who is omnipresent everywhere, and devoted to the Self, enter into Him wholly. (Mundakopanishad, iii. II. 5)

That, then, is the goal of this path of knowledge: a lofty state, supremely great, where a Soul, serene in its own strength and calm in its own wisdom, has stilled every impulse of the senses. It is absolute master over every movement of the mind, dwelling within the nine-gate city of its abode, neither acting nor causing to act. It dwells in a state of isolation, though a state great in power and wisdom, great in absolute detachment from all that is transitory, and ready to enter into Brahman. And into Brahman such a Soul enters and gains its liberation, to remain in that union for age after age—a time human years cannot reckon, human thought cannot span—having reached what the Hindu calls *moksha*, in perfect unity with the One and the All. Such a Soul comes out of that union only when the great manvantara redawns and life again passes into manifested forms.

The Path of Devotion

On the path of devotion, right knowledge may not be ignored. Right knowledge is needed for the world to be well served. Right knowledge is needed because union must be the goal, although a union somewhat different from that which is gained by knowledge. If right knowledge is absent, then even love may go astray in its desire of service and may injure where it would help. We must not have devotion unwedded to knowledge, for knowledge is needed for perfect service, and perfect service is the essence of the life of the devotee.

The goal of the path of devotion is conscious union with the supreme Self, which is recognized as manifesting through all other selves. Thought of those other selves persists until the union of all selves is found in the One. For in this path of devotion, love is the impulse, the love that is ever seeking to give itself—to those above it, to gain strength for service, and to those below to serve them. True devotees have their faces turned upward to those higher than themselves to gain spiritual force, spiritual strength, spiritual energy. This is not for themselves so that they may be liberated, for they desire no liberation until all share the freedom. It is not in order to gain, for they desire no gain except for giving. It is not that they may keep anything, but to be channels of blessing to others. On the path of devotion the Soul is ever turned to the Light above, not that it may be enlightened, not that it may shine, but that it may serve as focus and channel for that Light, to pass it on to those who are in darkness. It longs for the Light above only to pass it on to those below.

That, then, is the first, the supreme characteristic of those who would follow the path of devotion. They must begin in love, as in love they end. In order that this may be, they must recognize the spiritual side of nature, that they will not be alone. It is not enough to recognize the Self, to recognize the One of whom all forms are but passing manifestations. Devotees must recognize those passing manifestations in order to be equipped for service.

They will begin by recognizing that out of the One Eternal Source of Life—the Self of all—come the various sparks that are spiritual Intelligences in every grade of evolution. Some are mighty spiritual Intelligences that have gained victory in past manvantaras and come out of the eternal Fire ready to be lights in the world. These will be recognized as the supreme embodiments of the spiritual life and as the foundations of the manifested universe. Devotees will see these Beings as far, far above themselves; for evolution has carried Them onwards through many nirvanas to the place at which They emerge for the manifestations of our own universe. These great Ones will be given some name that carries with it their supreme spiritual greatness, so that one realizes in Them the supreme embodiments of spiritual life, towards whom the universe is tending and in union with whom it finds itself on the threshold of the One.

Stretching downwards from these great Ones in countless hierarchies are grade after grade of spiritual Intelligences in all the manifested forms of life in the spiritual side of the universe. They stretch downwards continually through the mighty Ones we speak of as Builders of the Worlds, Planetary Spirits, Lords of Wisdom, downwards from them to those great Ones embodied in the highest forms of humanity, the Masters, who reveal to us the divine Light that is beyond themselves. Lower and lower grades of spiritual entities stretch downwards until the whole universe is full of these living forms of Light and Life.

This hierarchy is recognized as one mighty brotherhood of whom embodied humans form part. Therefore the path is in the realization of brotherhood, and not in isolation. It is not liberation that devotees ask. They claim power of service from the Highest, in order to help those who have not yet reached the place where they themselves stand. Therefore the path of devotion begins in love to every sentient creature around us and ends in love to the Highest, the highest that our thought may conceive.

Recognizing this brotherhood of helpers, devotees would be conscious helpers with Them—taking their share in the burden of the universe, bearing their part of the common burden, and desiring more strength to use in the common helping, more wisdom to use in enlightening ignorance. They always seek to serve, and recognize the selves without as well as the Self within.

Those on the path of devotion realize renunciation, as do those on the path of knowledge, but their renunciation is of a different kind. It is not the stern renunciation of knowledge, which says, "I will not bind myself by attachment to transitory things, because they will bring me back to birth." It is the joyous renunciation of those who see beyond themselves the mighty helpers of humanity, and who, desiring to serve Them, cannot care for anything that holds them back. These devotees offer all to Them—not sternly, in order to be free, joyously to give everything to Them. They do not cut out desire with an axe, as you might cut the chain that binds you, but burn up desire in the fire of devotion, because that fire burns up everything that is not one with its heat and flame.

Such servers are free from karma, free because they desire nothing except to serve, to help, to reach union with their Lord and union with humanity. This service will indeed detach them from the senses and the mind, but the detachment will be to serve better. For this is the lesson learned by devotees: It is our duty to act, because without action the world could not go on; it is our duty to act in the very spot where we are because there lies the duty for which we have been born and which we should discharge perfectly.

Yet devotees do not seek the fruit of action. Realizing that we are here for action, they will act, but not so much for themselves. Their thought will be fixed on the subject of service and love, and as Sri Krishna said in the *Gita*, the senses and the mind will move to their appropriate objects, while we remain unfettered within.

The Wiser Ones Above Us

If we do our best and wisest work, if for love's sake we give our best thought and our best effort to the service of humanity, then the moment the act is accomplished we have no desire as to the result, except for it to be as the wiser Ones above us will and guide. We cut ourselves free from the action; doing our share in it, but leaving to Them an unfettered field where all great spiritual energies may play, unbarred and untouched by our blindness and weakness. We take no further interest in the result. Thus we leave Them to make our weakness perfect by their strength, to correct our blunders by their wisdom, our errors by their righteousness. The blunders that we make lose most of their power for mischief; though we shall reap pain for mistakes the issue will be right, for the desire was to serve. If we do not mix our own personality with it, then even out of our blunder will come success; the failure, being a failure of the intellect only, will give way before the mightier forces of the Spirit which is moved by love.

Then all anxiety disappears. The life which is at peace within in this devotion has no anxiety in the outer world. It does its best, and if it blunders it knows that pain will teach it of its blunder. It is glad to take the pain which teaches wisdom and so makes it more fit to be coworker with the great Souls who are the workers of the world. The pain for the blunder causes no distress; the pain for the error is seen as only a lesson. Taken thus, it cannot ruffle the Soul's serenity which wills only to learn to do right, and does not care what price it pays if it becomes a better servant of humanity and of our great Teachers.

Doing our best and leaving the results, we find that what we call devotion is really an attitude of the Soul. It is the attitude of love, the attainment of peace, which—having its face always turned to the Light of Those within—is always ready for service. By their light it finds fresh opportunities of service day by day.

Devotion to Whom?

You may say: To whom is this devotion paid? The root of this devotion must be found by each of us where we are, in devotion to those who are living around us. Talk of devotion is worth nothing if it does not show in a life of love. And that life of love must begin where love will be helpful to the nearest. True devotees are ones who, just because they have no thought or care for self, have thought and care for those around them. They are able, out of the great peace of their own selflessness, to find room for all the troubles and strifes of their fellows. So the life of devotion will begin in the home, in the perfect discharge of all duties in the home. The life of devotees shines in all the brightness that can be brought into home life, in bearing all the home burdens, in lightening every burden for others and taking them on oneself.

Then devotion moves from the life of the home to the life of the wider world, giving one's best there. Devotees never ask: Is it troublesome? Is it painful? Would I rather do something else? For their only will is to serve; and the best that they can give is that which they will to give.

Out of that life of service—first to the nearest and then to those farther away—comes the purifying fire of devotion which will make clearer our vision of Those who lie beyond and above. For only as we serve and love those around us will the eyes of the Spirit begin to open. Then we will recognize that there are helpers beyond ready to help us as we help others.

On this path of devotion there is no help given to the individual as an individual; it is only given by the Great Ones beyond if in our turn we pass it on to others. Our claim to be helped is that we are always helping. Therefore a gift to us individually is a gift to everyone that needs.

As our eyes become clearer and we recognize these many grades of Spiritual Intelligences, we will realize that some of them are embodied around us. By recognizing Those that are greater than ourselves, we will be able to climb upward step by step until we see the yet greater Ones beyond these; and the greater Ones still beyond. For in this path of spiritual progress by way of devotion, every step opens up new horizons. Every clearing of spiritual vision makes it pierce more deeply into that intensity of Light in which the highest Spiritual Intelligences are shrouded from the eyes of the flesh and the intellect. So the Soul of the devotee will gladly recognize all human excellence and love and admire that excellence wherever it is. Devotees may be hero-worshippers, not in seeing no fault in admired ones, but in seeing the good in them and loving that, and letting recognition of the good overbear criticism of faults. Devotees love and serve those they admire for what they are, and look with charity at their faults.

As devotees see and recognize excellence in those around them, they will come into touch with disciples higher than those who commonly move in the world, those who have reached a little farther, seen a little deeper. They will contact Spirits who are gradually burning up all ignorance and all selfishness, and who are in direct touch with Those whom we call the Masters, the members of the great White Lodge. Devotees will love and serve these disciples to the utmost of their ability if opportunity arises, knowing that all such service purifies us as well as helping the world, and makes us more and more a channel for energies we desire to spread among those with less vision than ourselves. After a while, through these, devotees come into touch with the Masters, those highest and mightiest embodiments of humanity. They are high above us in spiritual purity, in spiritual wisdom, in perfect selflessness. They seem as gods in comparison with lower humanity, because every sheath in Them is translucent, and the Light of the Spirit shines through unchecked. They are not different from us in their essence, but in their evolution. For the sheaths in us shroud the Light within us, while the sheaths with Them are pure.

The Masters help and guide and teach, when the devotee has risen to their feet by this path of devotion. Being in touch with Them is going forward on the path of spiritual

knowledge, for without devotion the further heights may
not be won.

The words of a Master of an Indian disciple gives the
meaning of devotion far better than any words of mine. He
wrote:

> Devotion to the Blessed Ones is a *sine qua non* of all spiritual
> progress and spiritual knowledge. It gives you the proper at-
> titude in which to work on all the planes of life. It creates the
> proper atmosphere for the soul to grow and flower in love
> and beauty, in wisdom and power. It tunes the harp of the
> heart, and thus makes it possible for the musician to play the
> correct notes. That is the function of devotion. But you must
> know the notes you have to play, your fingers must learn how
> to sweep along the strings, and you must have a musical ear,
> or better still, a musical heart. . . . What is proper tuning
> to the musical instrument, that devotion is to the human
> Monad. But other faculties are needed for the production of
> various sweet strains.

There is the meaning of devotion in a few words. It is the
tuning of the heart. Knowledge may be needed for the different strains that are wanted, but devotion tunes the heart
and the Soul, so that every strain may come out in perfect
harmony. Then comes the growth in love, the growth in
knowledge, the growth in spiritual purity. All the forces of
the spiritual spheres are helping this Soul that would rise for
service, and all the strength of Those who have achieved is
used to help the one who would achieve, in order that he or
she may serve better.

The Meaning of Devotion

What does devotion mean in life? It means clearer vision
so that we may see the right; it means deeper love so that
we may serve better; it means unruffled peace and calm so
that nothing can shake or disturb us, because, fixed on the
Blessed Ones in devotion, there is nothing that can touch the
Soul. Through those Blessed Ones shines the Light which
comes from beyond Them, which They focus to help the
worlds. They make it possible for our weak eyes to bear the
radiance.

And there are the peace, the vision, the power of service
—that is what devotion means in life. The Self that spotless
devotees seek is pure; that Self is Light (Mundakopanishad,
iii. I. 10)—Light which no soil may sully, Light no selfishness may dim, until the devotees vanish in the Light which
is themselves, for the very Self of all is Light and Love. The
time comes at last, which has come to the Masters, when
that Light shines out through spotless, transparent purity
and gives its full effulgence to help the world. That is the
meaning of devotion. That, however feebly phrased—and
all words are feeble—is the inner life of those who love, who
recognize that life is meant for service, that the only thing
that makes it worthwhile is to burn it in the fire of devotion,
so that the world may be lighted and warmed.

That is the goal which ends, not in liberation, but in
perfect service. Liberation comes only when all are liberated, when all enter into the bliss unspeakable, and which,
when that period of bliss is over, brings them out again as
conscious coworkers with unbroken memory in the higher
spiritual regions. For they have won their right to be conscious workers forever in all future manvantaras. The life
of love never trades liberation from service. As long as eternity endures, the Soul that loves works for and serves the
universe.

5

The Ceasing of Sorrow

The *Bhagavad Gita,* defining pleasure as threefold, says there is a pleasure "born of the blissful knowledge of the Self" that "putteth an end to pain" (xviii. 36, 37). Pleasures are many, but "the delights that are contact-born, they are verily wombs of pain," whereas only the one "whose self is unattached to external contacts . . . enjoys happiness exempt from decay" (v. 11, 12).

Looking at the faces we pass daily, in the city, or suburb, or the bus or train, of old, middle-aged and young people, of men and women, even too often of little ones—we see in them dissatisfaction and harassment, trouble and unrest. Rarely are we gladdened by a serene and happy face, free from lines carved by worry and anxiety, a face that tells of a Soul at peace with itself and with all around, of "a heart at leisure," unhurried, strong. There must be some cause for this general characteristic that increases with the increase of "civilization." Yet it is an avoidable evil, as evidenced by the rare sweet presences with a serener atmosphere who radiate peace as others radiate unrest.

A trouble so general must have its roots deep in human nature, and some fundamental principle, lying as deep as the trouble, must exist as remedy. There must be some mistake into which we fall that stamps on us this mark of sorrow. If this is so, then ignorance brings about our sadness, and knowledge of the mistake would put the remedy within our grasp.

Ages ago this knowledge was given in the *Upanishads;* somewhat less than five thousand years ago it was expounded in the original *Bhagavad Gita;* twenty-four centuries ago the Lord Buddha presented the immemorial teaching in plainest language; nineteen hundred years ago the Christ offered the same gift to the Western world. Some, learning it, have entered the supreme peace; some, earnestly striving to learn it, are feeling its distant touch as an ever-growing reality; some, seeing its far-off radiance through a momentary rift in the storm clouds, yearningly aspire to reach it. But the myriads of driven souls do not know of it or even dream of it. Yet this knowledge is not far from any of us. Perhaps repeating the ancient teaching may help one here and there to escape from sorrow's net, to break the connection with pain.

The Cause of Sorrow

The cause of sorrow is the thirst for the separated life in which individuality begins. Without that thirst the eternal seed could not become a center of self-consciousness able to exist amid the tremendous vibrations which disintegrate universes. That seed would not be able to remain without a circumference, with the power to generate one again and again, and thus to act as an axis for the eternal Motion when it is going to turn the great wheel for a new "pilgrimage thereon." Unless the thirst for separated life were aroused, universes could never come into manifestation. This thirst must continue in each Soul until it has accomplished its mighty task—a paradox to the intellect but a truism to the spirit—of forming a center which is eternal and at the same time is everything.

While this thirst for separated life again and again draws the soul into the ocean of births and deaths, a still deeper constituent of its being drives it to seek union. We all seek happiness, if blindly. The search needs no justification; it is a universal instinct. Even those who torture the body and seem to trample on happiness choose the valley of pain only because they believe that it is the shortest path to a deeper and more abiding joy.

Now what is the essence of happiness, found alike in the passion of the sensualist and in the ecstasy of the saint? It is union with the object of desire, becoming one with that which promises delight. The drunkard who swallows his drink, the miser who clutches his gold, the lover who embraces his beloved, the artist who saturates herself in beauty, the thinker who concentrates on his idea, the mystic who loses herself in the empyrean, the yogi who merges in Deity—all are finding happiness in union with the object of desire. But their place in evolution is shown by the object with which they seek union. The distinguishing mark of a base or lofty Soul is not the search for happiness, but the nature of the object which yields happiness.

The Life Within Forms

In any given universe One Life is evolving into many lives through an ascending series of forms. The lives manifest as energies, displayed and further developed by means of forms. In order that these lives may thus develop, the forms must continually change, for each form is first an instrument and later a prison. As the latent powers in a life—ever inseparable from the One Life as a plant from its hidden root—are drawn out by the play of the environment upon it, the form which was its helpful vehicle becomes a mold that cramps it. Either the life must perish, stifled by the form it had shaped, or the form must break into pieces and set free the life in an embryonic form of a higher type. But the life cannot perish, being an offshoot of the Eternal. Hence the form must break. The breaking of a series of forms around an ever-expanding life means evolution.

The expansion of this life may be likened to the expansion of life in a seed—from nucleus to embryo, from embryo to seedling, from seedling to sapling, from sapling to tree, capable of yielding seeds like that from which it grew. All growth is the unfolding of hidden powers, powers that in a Logos reached their highest point for that universe—his universe—powers He plants as seed of every separated life. As water ever rises to its own level, so does this life that is poured down strive to rise to the level of its source; as mass attracts mass so does each life that is separate in manifestation seek the One Life. That One Life ceaselessly exerts an upward drawing force. The embryonic Self in each answers

to the One Self and blindly reaches out, groping after that
One within the many, the One that is itself.

Thus external contacts arise. The forms meet by the inward urging of the Self, then cling or clash. The attractive
force is the one Self in all; the variety, the pleasure or the
pain, is in the forms.

Further, the life in one form seeks the life in another
form. But the form finds only the form of others, thus baf-
fling the seeker. The forms are barriers between life and
life; they cannot intermingle and are mutually exclusive.
Life could mix with life as two rivers mix their waters, but
as rivers cannot join while each is running within its own
banks, so lives cannot unite while forms lock each life
within its own enclosure.

Let us gather up our threads and twist them together to
guide us through the labyrinth of life so that we may overcome sorrow:

> A thirst for separated life is necessary to build one who
> endures.
> There is persistent seeking for happiness.
> The essence of happiness lies in union with the object of
> desire.
> One Life is evolving through many impermanent forms.
> Each separated life seeks this Life which is itself, and thus
> forms come into contact.
> These forms exclude each other and keep the contained lives
> apart.

We may now understand how sorrow arises. A Soul seeks
beauty and finds a beautiful form; it unites itself to the
form, rejoices over it; the form perishes and a void is left. A
Soul seeks love and finds a lovable form; it unites itself to the
form and finds joy in it; the form perishes and the heart is
desolate.

But even uniting with a form and losing it are less painful
than satiety, than relinquishing a hard-won prize, than disillusion on the heels of disillusion, but with ever fresh illusion and ever renewed disgust.

Search the world over and we find that all the suffering of
normal evolution is due to union with changing and dying
forms, that the blind and foolish seek enduring happiness by

clinging to forms that perish. These are the *Gita*'s "delights that are contact-born." Because they lead to weariness, or at best to loss, they are truly described as "wombs of pain."

Against these we are bidden to seek "the blissful knowledge of the Self." Let life seek Life, and the way to happiness is found: let the self seek the Self, and the path winding up to peace stretches before one. To seek happiness by union with forms is to dwell in the transitory, the limited, the clashing; to seek happiness by union with Life is to rest at peace on the permanent, the infinite, the harmonious.

Does this sound as though we are stripping our lives of joy and beauty, and making them lonely in measureless depths of space? It is not so, for what we love in our beloved is not the form but the life, not the body but the Soul. Clear-eyed love can leap across death's abyss, across birth's Lethe-stream, and find and clasp its own unerringly, though a new and alien form serves as casket for the jewel-soul it knows. When we see this, we understand the cause of sorrow. For we, ourselves life not form, unite our life to life, not form, in our dear ones. We blend with them more and more, as form after form is dashed in pieces by the compassionate severity of a law that is love. Eventually we find ourselves not two but one, one also with the Life that is in and around and through all. Though amid the separated we are not separate. We have put an end to pain. This is the ceasing of sorrow, the entering into peace.

On the way to bliss, moreover, understanding the cause of sorrow robs sorrow of its sting. We learn that it seems stern only because it is veiled happiness "which at first is as venom but in the end is as nectar." From this knowledge springs a strong serenity that can endure as though seeing the end, can "glorify the Lord in the fires." Should not gold rejoice in the burning that frees it from worthless dross?

If we did not experience sorrow, we could not develop strength. Strong mental and moral muscles are not obtained without strenuous exercise, any more than physical muscles become powerful without it. Struggle is a condition of the lower evolutions in Nature; it is the means by which strength is developed. Only perfect strength is calm.

If we did not experience sorrow, we could not evolve sympathy. By suffering we learn to understand both the pain and its needs, the demand and how to meet it. Having been tempted we learn how to help effectively others who are tempted; only those who have risen from falls can aid the fallen with that exquisite understanding that alone prevents help from being insulting. Every bud of pain opens into a blossom of power. Who would begrudge the brief travail that brings forth a savior?

Without the experience of sorrow, we could not gain the knowledge of good and evil. Without this our conscious choice of the highest could not become certain, nor the root of desire to unite with forms be eradicated. The lower nature of those who are perfect does not still yearn for delights of the senses, but is strongly held in check. Such perfected ones have eliminated from their lower nature all its own tendencies, and have brought it into perfect harmonious union (yoga) with themselves. They pass through the lower worlds unaffected by attractions or repulsions, their will unalterably pointing towards the highest, working without effort, with all the inviolability of law and all the flexibility of intelligent adaptation. Hundreds of incarnations are not too many, myriad years are not too long to build such a person.

Never let us forget, in the wildest storm of sorrow, that these early stages of our evolution in which pain plays so large a part are only early stages. They are an infinitesimal proportion of our existence, or rather the two things are incommensurables, for how can we measure time against eternity, myriad years against an unending life? If we spoke of the cycle of reincarnation as the infant stage of humanity, full of infantile ailments, we would exaggerate its relative importance, for "our light affliction, which is but for a moment, worketh for us a far more exceeding and eternal weight of glory." Therefore when the storm clouds gather, look beyond them to the changeless sky; when the billows buffet, lift your eyes to the eternal shore. Even the angriest forces that overwhelm us shall only lift us upwards, bear us onwards. For we are unborn, undying, constant, changeless and eternal, and we are here only to forge instruments for an immortal service, the service which is perfect freedom.

6

The Value of Devotion

Among the many forces which inspire us to activity, perhaps none plays a greater part than the feeling we call devotion, along with some feelings that often mask themselves under its name though fundamentally differing from it in essence. The most heroic self-sacrifices have been inspired by devotion, while the most terrible sacrifices of others have been brought about by its pseudo-sister fanaticism. Devotion is as powerful a lever for raising us as is fanaticism for degradation. The two sway humanity with overwhelming power, and in some of their manifestations they appear to resemble one another. But one has its roots in knowledge, the other in ignorance; one bears the fruits of love, the other the poison apples of hate.

A clear understanding of the nature of devotion is necessary, before we are in a position to weigh its value and to distinguish it from the false Duessa. We must trace it to its origin in human nature, and see in what part of that nature it takes its rise. We must know in order that we may practice; for as knowledge without practice is barren, so practice without knowledge is wasted. Emotion unregulated by knowledge, like a river overflowing its banks, spreads in every direction as a devastating flood, while emotion guided by knowledge is like the same river running in appointed channels and fertilizing the land through which it flows.

If we study the inner nature of humanity, we find that it readily reveals three marked aspects that are distinguished from each other as the spiritual, the intellectual, and the emotional. On studying these further, we learn that the spiritual nature is that in which all the separate individualities inhere. It is the common root, the unifying influence, that principle which, when developed, enables us to realize in consciousness the oneness of all that lives.

The intellectual nature may be said to be its antithesis. It is the individualizing force, that which makes the many from the One. Its self-realization is "I," and it sharply divides this from the "not-I." It knows itself apart, separate, and it works best in isolation, drawn inwards, self-concentrated, indifferent to what is without. The root of devotion, of a feeling which rushes outward, cannot be found here. The intellect can only grasp, it cannot move. The emotional nature is the energizing force that causes action, that which feels. This is what attracts us to an object or repels us from it, and we shall find that devotion has its source here.

The Root of Devotion

As we study the emotional nature we see that it has two aspects—attraction and repulsion. It is always moving us towards or away from objects surrounding us, according to whether those objects afford us pleasure or pain. All the feelings which draw us towards another fall under the heading of attraction and are forms of love. All those which repel us from another fall under the heading of repulsion and are forms of hate.

Now love takes different forms and is called by different names, depending on whether its object is above it, equal with it, or below it. Directed to those below, we name it pity, compassion, benevolence; directed to those equal with it, we call it friendship, passion, affection; directed to those above, we style it reverence, adoration, devotion. Thus we trace devotion to its origin in the love-side of the emotional nature, and we define it as love directed to an object superior to the lover. When love is directed to the guru or to God, we rightly term it devotion. For then it is poured out to a superior, and shows the characteristic of all love given to those who are greater than ourselves, self-surrender.

Here we have the touchstone by which we can separate devotion from the fanaticism which has inspired religious

wars, religious persecutions, religious animosities. These
have their roots in hatred, not in love; they repel us from
others instead of drawing us toward them. In the name of
love of God, people injure their fellows. But when we ana-
lyze the motive of their actions we do not find it is love but
their sense that they are right and others wrong, in the separateness they feel from others, in the feeling of repulsion
from them because of their supposed wrongness. The root of
fanaticism is hate. Out of this come the bitter waters that
sterilize the heart over which they flow. We can judge what
we regard as devotion in ourselves by this: if it makes us
humble, gentle, tolerant, friendly to all, then it is true devotion; if it makes us proud, harsh, separate, suspicious of all,
then, however fair it may seem, it is dross, not gold.

Now devotion, being a form of love, can flow out only
when an object attractive in its own nature, presents itself,
one that gives happiness. All people seek happiness, and
anything attracts them and draws them towards itself, that
seems to make for happiness. Happiness is the feeling which
accompanies the increase of life. All efforts toward happiness are efforts to unite with objects in order to absorb
their life, thereby expanding the life that absorbs them.
Happiness results from this union, because the feeling of life
is increased.

Fundamentally the impulse to seek union comes from the
Self, seeking to overcome the barriers which separate its
selves on the lower planes. The attraction between selves is
the Self in each seeking the Self in the other. "Lo, not for the
sake of the husband is the husband dear, but for the sake of
the Self the husband is dear. Lo! not for the sake of the wife
is the wife dear, but for the sake of the Self the wife is dear."
And so also with sons, wealth, Brahmanas, Kshattriyas, the
worlds, the gods, the Vedas, the elements, until, "Lo! not
for the sake of the All is the All dear, but for the sake of the
Self the All is dear." (Brihadaranyakopanishad, VI. v. 6)
The Self seeks the Self, and this is the universal search for
happiness, frustrated by the clash of form with form, the
obstruction of the vehicles in which the separated selves
abide. True and permanent bliss lies in union with the Self,

the All-life, in conscious Self-identification with and expansion into the All.

Objects of Devotion

Attractive objects are necessary to draw out devotion. Such objects are presented most completely in the revelations of the Supreme Self made through human form in the divine Incarnations who appear from time to time—the Avataras. Such beings are rendered supremely attractive by the beauty of character they manifest, by the rays of the Self which shine through the human veil, imperfectly concealing their divine loveliness. When ones who are beauty and love and bliss show a portion of themselves on earth, encased in human form, our weary eyes light up, and our tired hearts expand with a new hope, a new vigor. We are irresistibly attracted to these great ones, and devotion spontaneously springs up.

Among Christians the intensity of religious devotion flows out to Christ, the Divine Man, regarded as an incarnation of Deity, far more than to "God" in the abstract. It is his human side, his life and death, his sympathy and compassion, his gentle wisdom and patient sufferings, which stir hearts to a passion of devotion; as the Man of Sorrows, the innocent and willing sufferer, he perennially wins love; the memory of him as human holds Christians captive. As phrased by one of his devotees:

> The cross of Christ
> Is more to us than all His miracles.

It is the same with Saviors in other faiths. Sri Rama the divine king and Sri Krishna the friend and lover win the undying passionate devotion of millions of human hearts. They render Deity attractive by softening its dazzling radiance into a light that human eyes can bear as it shines through the veil of humanity. They limit the divine attributes till they become small enough for human intelligence to grasp. These stand as objects of devotion, attracting love by their perfect loveableness. They need only to be seen to be loved; if They are not loved, it is merely because They have not been seen.

Devotion to divine Incarnations is not a matter for discussion or argument. The moment one of Them is seen by the inner vision, the heart rushes out and falls unbidden at his feet. Devotion may be cultivated by the reason and may be approved of and nurtured by the intelligence. But its primary impulse comes from the heart, not from the head, and flows out spontaneously to the object that attracts it, to the shining of the Self through a translucent veil.

Next, as objects of devotion, come the Teachers who, having Themselves obtained liberation, remain voluntarily within touch of humanity, retaining human bodies while they enjoy nirvanic consciousness on higher planes. They stand, as it were, between the Avataras and the earthly gurus who are their disciples. These gurus have not yet reached liberation, but to those on earth they are scarcely distinguishable from the Avataras, and draw people with the same overwhelming attraction. The Avatara truly is greater than a Master, but that greatness lies on the side turned away from earth, and we can imagine no more complete perfection than that of the Masters of Wisdom.

Then, in more constant physical communication with us, come the gurus who are the immediate spiritual teachers of those on the steep path that leads to human perfection. Though still marred by weaknesses, these gurus have advanced sufficiently beyond their fellows to serve as their guides and helpers, and for the most part the earlier stages of progress are trodden by devotion to them. They are near the threshold of liberation and will shortly pass into the class beyond themselves. Then, as spiritual links are imperishable, they will be able to draw their devotees after them with added force. Love given to them strengthens and expands the nature of their devotees, and there is no surer path of devotion, in its highest meaning, than the love and trust given to an earthly guru.

Nowhere has this been realized so strongly as in the East, where the love and service of the guru have always been held as necessary to spiritual progress. Much of the decay of modern India is due to the ignorance, the pride, the unspirituality of those who still wear the ancient name while devoid of all the qualities it once implied. For as the best wine makes the sharpest vinegar, so the degradation of the highest reaches the lowest depth.

How, then, shall devotion be evoked and nourished? Only by meeting a fit object of devotion in the outer or inner world and by yielding fully and unreservedly to the attraction it exerts. Cordially recognizing excellence wherever found, checking the critical, carping spirit that fixes on defects and ignores virtues, these prepare the Soul to recognize the guru when he or she appears. For many miss their teacher by the mental habit of fixing the attention on blemishes rather than on beauties, by seeing only the sun spots and not the Sun. Further, recognizing excellence shows the capacity to reproduce it; sympathetic vibrations are given out only by a string tuned to produce by itself a similar note. The soul knows its kin, even though they are older; only those akin to greatness are awakened to response by the great.

When the guru is found and the tie is made, the first great step is taken. Then follows the steady culture of devotion to the guru, and through him or her to Those beyond and to the Supreme Self, manifested in form. But we must remember that the guru is a means not an end, a transmitter not an originator of the divine Light, a moon not a sun. Gurus help, strengthen, guide and evolve their pupils, but the end is the Self shining out in the disciple, the Self that is one and is in guru and disciple alike.

Nourishing Devotion

Devotion to the embodiment of the Self as Avataras may be nourished and increased by reading and meditating on their sayings and the incidents of their lives on earth. It is a good plan to read over an incident and then vividly picture it in your mind, using your imagination to produce a full and detailed picture, and to feel yourself present in it as a spectator or an actor. This deliberate use of the imagination provokes devotion. It actually brings devotees into touch with the scene depicted, so that they may one day find themselves scanning the akashic record of the event. They will be a part of that living picture, learning undreamed of lessons from their presence there.

Another way to cultivate devotion is to spend time in the company of those in whom devotion burns more brightly than in ourselves. As burning wood thrown into a smoldering fire will cause a flame to burst out brightly again, so being near the warm fire of devotion in another rekindles the flagging energy of a weaker Soul. Here again, the disciple may gain much by frequenting the company of the guru, whose steadier force will energize his or her own. The ancient Indian sage, Narada, in his admirable sutras, thus instructs us on the culture of devotion, and who should teach better than that ideal devotee?

It is almost needless to add that contemplating, meditating on, adoring the object of devotion quicken and intensify the love. In the hurry of modern life, we are apt to forget the power of quiet thought and to begrudge the time necessary for its exercise. Thinking of the one we love increases love, so that would-be devotees must give time to the object of their devotion. And it is not their thought alone that is at work. As a plant cannot grow without sunlight, so devotion cannot grow without the warming and energizing rays that stream from its object. The older Souls pour out far more love than they receive, and their light and heat permeate and strengthen the younger Soul. The guru loves the disciple and God loves the devotee far more than the disciple loves the guru or the devotee loves God. The love of the devotee for his or her Lord is but a faint reflection of the love of One who is Love itself. It is said that if a child throws a pebble to the ground, the whole great earth moves towards the pebble as well as drawing the pebble to itself. Attraction cannot be one-sided. In the spiritual world when we take one step towards God, God takes a hundred steps towards us; the ocean pours forth its measureless depths towards any drop that seeks its bosom.

The Value of Devotion

Having seen what devotion is, what its objects are, how it can be increased, we may fitly measure its value so as to find a motive for attaining it.

Devotion changes devotees into the likeness of the one they love. Solomon, the wise Hebrew, declared that as a man thinks so is he. The *Chhandogyopanishad* teaches that we are created by thought; what we think on that we become. But the intellect alone cannot easily be shaped into the likeness of the Supreme. As cold iron is hard and incapable of being worked, but heated in the furnace becomes fluid and flows readily into any desired mold, so it is with the intellect. It must be melted in the fire of devotion, and then it will quickly be shaped into the likeness of the Beloved. Even love between equals, when it is strong and faithful and long continued, molds them into each other's likeness: husband and wife become like each other, close friends grow similar to each other. Love directed to one above us exercises its transforming power still more forcibly, and easily shapes the nature it renders plastic into likeness of that which is enshrined in the heart.

Devotion prevents making new karma, and when the old karma is exhausted the devotee is free. St. Paul declared that he no longer lived, but Christ lived in him. This saying becomes true for devotees as their devotion leads to surrender utterly to the one they love. They think of their body not as theirs, but as an instrument used by their Lord to help the world. All their actions are done as duty for the Beloved. They eat, not to gratify the palate, but to keep their Lord's instrument in working order. They think, not for the pleasure of thinking, but that their Lord's work may be done better. Devotees merge their life in the life they love, think, work, act in union with that higher life, merging their smaller channel of being in the larger stream, and finding a deep joy in feeling part of the fuller life. So it is written: "Whatsoever thou doest, whatsoever thou eatest, whatsoever thou offerest, whatsoever thou givest, whatsoever thou doest of austerity, O son of Kunti, do thou that as an offering unto Me. Thus shalt thou be liberated from the bonds of action [yielding] good and evil fruits" (*Bhagavad-Gita*, ix. 27, 28). Where fruits of action are not desired, where actions are done only as sacrifice, no karma is made by the actor, and one is not bound by them to the wheel of births and deaths.

Devotion cleanses the heart. Sri Krishna teaches us with words that at first seem strange, "Even if the most sinful worship me with undivided heart, he too must be accounted righteous." Why? we naturally ask. "Because he hath rightly resolved; *speedily he becometh dutiful*, and goeth to peace eternal" (*Bhagavad-Gita*, 30, 31). In the higher world we are judged by motives not by actions, by inner attitude not by external signs. When we feel devotion to the Supreme, we turn our back on evil and turn our face to the goal; we may stumble, stray, even fall, but our face is turned in the right direction, we are going homewards. The force of devotion makes us dutiful. For seeking union with the Beloved we swiftly cast away everything that prevents the union. To one who sees the end from the beginning we are righteous when our face is turned to righteousness. Our love will burn up the evil that veils the one we adore and produce in ourselves the likeness we worship. This action is so sure, the law so inviolable that we are "accounted righteous." We have changed from self-seekers to seekers of the Self.

Devotion puts an end to pain. What we do for the object of our love is done with joy, and pain is merged in gladness when it is endured for the sake of the Beloved. The earthly lover will gladly undergo hardships, perils, sufferings to win approval from his beloved or to gain something desirable for her. Those who have caught a glimpse of the beauty of the Self joyfully do anything that brings them nearer to union. They sacrifice ungrudgingly, even with delight, all that withholds them from union with the loved one. For the sake of being with one we love, we readily endure inconvenience, sacrifice comfort, the joy of the presence of the loved one lends charm to surmounting obstacles that separate us. Thus devotion makes hard things easy and painful things pleasant. For love is an alchemist that transmutes all to gold.

Devotion gives peace. The heart at peace in the Self is at peace with all. Devotees see the Self in all; all forms around them bear the impress of the Beloved. How then can they hate or despise or repel anyone when the face they love smiles at them behind every mask? "Sages look with equal eye on a Brahmana adorned with learning and humility, on a cow, an elephant, and even a dog and a dog-eater" (*Bhagavad-Gita*, v. 18). No one, nothing, can be outside the heart of devotees," since nothing is outside the embrace of their Lord. If we love the very objects touched by the one we love, how shall we not love all forms in which the Beloved is enshrined? A child in play may place a hideous mask over his laughing face, but the mother knows her darling is underneath. When in the world-lila or play the Lord is hidden under repulsive forms, devotees are not repelled, but see only the Beloved. There is no creature, moving or unmoving, that exists bereft of the Lord, and in the heart-chamber of the vilest sinner the Holiest abides.

Thus we return to our starting-point and learn to recognize devotees by their attitudes toward their fellow-creatures. Their abounding love, their tenderness, compassion, pity, sympathy with all faiths and all ideals, these mark them out as lovers of the Lord of Love. It is told of Sri Ramanujacharya that a mantra was once given him by his guru, and he asked what would happen if he told it to another. "Thou wilt die," was the answer. "And what will happen to the one who hears it?" "He will be liberated." Then the devotee of Sri Krishna ran out, and flying to the top of a tower, he shouted out the mantra to the crowded streets below, careless of what happened to himself, wanting only that others be set free from sin and sorrow. There is the typical devotee, there the lover transformed into the likeness of the Beloved.

7

Spiritual Darkness

Few of the perils that beset the path of the serious aspirant are more depressing, more fatal in their effects, than what is called spiritual darkness—the gloom that descends on the heart and brain, wrapping one's whole nature in its somber folds, blotting out memories of past peace, hopes of future progress. As a dense fog pervades a great city, stealing into every corner, effacing every familiar landmark, dimming even the brilliant lights, until, to bewildered wayfarers, nothing seems left except themselves and the foul, stifling vapor that enfolds them—so is it when the fog of spiritual darkness comes down on aspirants or disciples. All their landmarks disappear, and the way vanishes in the gloom; their familiar lights lose luster, and human beings are mere shadows that now and again push up out of the night and disappear into the night again.

Aspirants are alone and lost; a sense of terrible isolation shuts them in, and no one shares their solitude. The faces that smiled on them have vanished; the voices that cheered them are silent: the love that caressed them has grown chill. Their "lovers and friends are put away" from them, and no words of comfort reach across the deadly stillness.

To move forward when the ground on which one's foot must be planted is invisible feels like stepping over a precipice. A dull surging of waves at a great depth seems to threaten destruction, while the waves' very depth intensifies the silence near the surface. Heaven is shut out as well as earth; sun, moon and stars have vanished, and no glimmer of their radiance pierces the gloom from above. Aspirants feel suspended in an abyss of nothingness, and as though they would shortly pass into that nothingness. Their flame of life seems to flicker in the darkness as though, in sympathy with the universal gloom, it would itself cease to shine. The "horror of great darkness" is upon them, paralyzing their energy, crushing their hope. God and humans have deserted them—they are alone.

The testimony of every great mystic proves that this picture is not overdrawn. There are no cries of human anguish more bitter than those from the pages on which saintly souls have recorded their experiences on the Path. They look for peace, but combat surrounds them; for joy, but find sorrow; for the Beatific Vision, but the darkness of the pit hems them in.

It proves nothing that lesser souls have not faced the ordeal, and look unbelievingly on its possibility. Their hour has not yet come. The child cannot measure the adult's struggle, nor the infant feel the anguish that pierces the breast that feeds it. Every age has its proper fruit, and while we can understand the experiences that lie behind us, we cannot grasp the nature of those that lie ahead. Let undeveloped souls scoff at the agony they cannot appreciate, depreciate the suffering they cannot yet feel, even deride as weakness the signs of an anguish whose lightest touch would shrivel up their strength. Those growing into divine maturity know the reality of the darkness, and only those who know can judge.

At a very early stage of real apprenticeship to the higher life, darkness—less absolute than that described, but trying enough—will strain and test the disciple's powers. Earnest aspirants soon find that fits of gloom, the cause of which they cannot discover, descend upon them causing much distress. In the oversensitiveness which accompanies this stage of growth, they are apt to blame themselves for these excesses of sadness, and to reprimand themselves for the loss of the serenity which is their ideal.

When the gloom is upon them, every object takes an unfamiliar and exaggerated shape. Small annoyances loom large, distorted by the surrounding mists; petty troubles grow into great shadows that cloud the sun; friction that in happier times would pass unnoticed now rasps every nerve.

Disciples feel that they have fallen from the place to which they had climbed by prolonged efforts, and that all their past struggles are wasted. As has been well said, "It is wonderful how the Powers of the Dark seem to sweep away, as it were, in one gust all one's spiritual treasures, garnered with such pain and care after years of incessant study and experience." Bewildered neophytes despair as their victory crumbles into ashes.

Causes of Darkness

Let us examine the cause of the darkness. While it is upon us, all merely theoretical knowledge breaks down, yet that knowledge may help to clear away the darkness more rapidly once it begins to lighten. Nothing but repeated practical experience can keep us as steady and serene in the darkness as in the light, but theoretical knowledge has its place in the evolution of the mind.

We will take separately the cases of the aspirant and of the disciple who has been accepted as apprentice by a Master. Though the causes of the darkness which affect the aspirant may also play their part in bringing the night on the disciple, there are additional causes at work with the accepted disciple.

First comes the well-known fact of the quickening of karma, once we have set our feet resolutely towards the portal of the Path. We need not dwell on this for it has been explained often, and it plays a comparatively small part in bringing on the darkness. One element, however, perhaps less often alluded to, may be mentioned here.

Pleasure and pain, connected with the emotions and passions, belong to the astral world and are experienced through the astral body; consequently a very large amount of karma belongs, by its very nature, to the astral plane, and is exhausted there. Bad karma can, therefore, be largely worked out by suffering, apart from events; the suffering that normally accompanies misfortunes and disasters of every description on the physical plane takes place on the astral; we suffer on the astral while we are passing through troubles on the physical. Now this astral suffering can be disjoined from the physical events with which it is normally associated, and can be passed through apart from those events.

In the quickening of karma this takes place, and some of the darkness experienced by aspirants is due to this cause; they are working out bad karma by enduring the suffering that belongs to events not yet ripe for manifestation on the physical plane. They will find that, later on, they pass through events that would ordinarily be most distressing with a surprising calmness and indifference. The fact is that they have already borne the suffering normally attached to such events, and on the physical plane meet the empty forms, which are all that remain when the astral consciousness that normally vivifies these forms has been withdrawn. (Students may be reminded—thought the subject is too large to be entered on here—that human consciousness is astral, at the present stage of evolution.) Therefore, when an apparently causeless gloom descends, aspirants may be comforted with the knowledge that they are exhausting some of their karmic liabilities, and that the payment of karmic debts is never demanded twice.

Second, aspirants are seeking to purify and ultimately destroy the personality. Pleasures increase and intensify the life of the personality, while pains diminish it. The aspirants' deliberate will has offered the personality as a sacrifice to the Lord, and if the sacrifice is accepted, the flame falls and devours it. What cause for sorrow here? But the fire, as it burns up the dross of personality setting free the pure gold of the life, brings keen suffering to the life which is thus rapidly purged from elements that have for millennia formed part of its being.

Can aspirants hold out while the dark fire burns up that which seems to be their very life? Can they bear the strain, live through the darkness, and be found, when it lifts, still at their post, weary and worn-out, but *there*? If they can, then a great peace will succeed the darkness. New strength will flow in upon them, and they will be conscious of a deeper vision, of a firmer grasp on truth. The darkness will prove to be the mother of light, and they will have learned in it priceless lessons for future trials. But too often courage breaks and endurance fails; the darkness proves a temporary tomb, perhaps for the remainder of that incarnation, bringing "ruin to many a noble soul that has not yet acquired strength enough to endure."

Third, the darkness is often a glamor thrown over the aspirant by the destructive forces that play in the world. Destruction is as necessary to the process of evolution as construction, disintegration as necessary as integration. That which apparently delays really strengthens. Occultists know that every force in nature represents the working of an invisible Intelligence, and that this is as true of destructive as of constructive forces. They know that the destructive Intelligences—the Dark Powers, as they are often called—set themselves to beguile, entrap and bewilder aspirants the moment they have made sufficient progress beyond ordinary humanity to draw attention and become worthy of attack. Endeavoring to delay the higher evolution and to prolong the sovereignty of matter, the Dark Powers regard as their natural enemy anyone who steps out of the normal path and seeks to lead the spiritual life.

These are the "powers of nature," so often mentioned in mystic books, who strive to hold back the aspiring soul. Their favorite device, perhaps, is to cause discouragement and, if possible, to drive aspirants to despair by enveloping them in darkness and making them feel forsaken and alone. Their touch gives peculiar poignancy to the isolation; thoughts that whisper of despair are the echoes of their mockery.

As progress is made on the Path, all the powers of nature must gradually be faced and conquered, and one must do the facing and the conquering alone. We are alone so far as the intellect is concerned, which feels the "I" as standing unaided and forlorn. But not alone in reality. What shall separate us from the One Life which is our very Self, or from the love of the Masters who watch our every step on the Path?

Sorrow for the World

When we study the life of accepted disciples, we find the causes we have seen in the life of aspirants, but a new cause also arises. As disciples advance, this plays a more and more prominent part in their experience. As the shackles of their own karma fall off, they become free to bear part of "the heavy karma of the world." They also begin to face the greater destructive forces for the world's sake, standing between these forces and humanity and drawing these energies to themselves as much as is practical. The sin and the sorrow of the world, its pathetic ignorance, press upon disciples, and until they reach the strong peace which has its root in perfect knowledge, they cannot escape, from time to time, the gloom which comes upon them, as though the whole world's sorrow crushed their heart, and made it bleed with pity for the blindness that breeds misery, the ignorance which is sin. They dare not strive to shake off this feeling of sorrow, since, because of the more and more realized unity of their life with that of all, their sorrow is humanity's, and they share in humanity's karma and quicken its evolution. But the disciple gradually learns to bear this sorrow with peaceful satisfaction that deepens into a sense of profound inner joy, until its crushing power diminishes and finally disappears. Only abounding compassion remains, so that the sorrow becomes dearer than all that the world calls joy, and the gloom is but a tender twilight, fairer and sweeter than the brilliance of the noonday sun.

The disciple faces sharper and keener suffering when he "turns his back on the light and goes down alone into the darkness to meet and overcome the Powers of Evil." This is the work of the world's Saviors, and the hour comes for disciples when this solemn duty devolves on them. They are trained for its more arduous struggles by gradually learning to draw inharmonious and disruptive forces into themselves, so that these forces become exhausted, often tearing and rending the disciple in the process. They are then sent forth harmonized and rhythmical, forces for building instead of for destroying. Disciples are the crucibles of nature; in them compounds that are mischievous are dissociated and recombined into compounds that promote the general good. As the compounds break up with explosive violence, the sensitive human crucible quivers under the strain, and at times breaks.

By such discipline, long-continued, disciples strengthen their power and become fit to bear heavier burdens, to bear the gloom of the darkness in which they feel forsaken by God and humans, in which they seem flung to the Dark Powers and life is only torture, and they crave loss of consciousness.

Then comes the subtle temptation, "Come down from the cross." Disciples know that only the nails of their own fixed purpose and indomitable will hold them there. At any moment they can stop the torment, if they are willing to escape at the cost of the world they have sacrificed themselves to help. If they escape, the world must suffer; if they can bear the agony, the burden of humanity is a little lifted. "He saved others; himself he cannot save." The gibe of the unbeliever is the law of the Christ.

But at last, even this hope is gone and the darkness of despair enfolds disciples, whispering that all the anguish is in vain, that they are beaten, and all their hoped-for service to the world is but the "baseless vision of a dream." They feel they will never serve the Master again or gladden souls by their light. Though they have taught others to tread the Path, they have fallen from it. Can they hold out through this and be content to perish if that is their karma? Can they rejoice that the world will be saved though they have no part in saving it, that love will triumph though they are cast from its embrace? If they cannot, then the darkness has stifled them, and the world has for a while lost a helper. If they can, then with the uttermost surrender of the separated self, the darkness lifts; the eternal Self wells up within; the face of the Master shines out and victorious disciples know that He has been there all the time. In a moment of clear spiritual vision, they see the Holy of Holies, and the peace enfolds them.

Then disciples rest briefly in the calm stillness before coming forth into a new and larger life, with deeper wisdom, firmer faith, stronger love, greater power to serve humanity, strength to endure still heavier strain. Above all they have learned something of the power of illusion and caught a glimpse of the nature of Maya, and that will help in future darkness. They realize that it cannot wreck them unless they yield to its delusive force. Such is the priceless fruit of spiritual darkness, and by such strain and struggle the human evolves the God.

8

The Meaning and Method of the Spiritual Life

In considering the meaning and the method of the spiritual life, it is well to begin by defining the meaning of the term "spiritual." There is a good deal of uncertainty about it. We hear "spirit" and "soul" spoken of as though they were interchangeable terms. We have "a body and soul," or "a body and spirit," people say, as though the two words "spirit" and "soul" had no definite and distinct meaning. Naturally, if these words are not clearly understood, the term "spiritual life" remains confused.

Theosophy divides the human constitution in a definite way, both as regards consciousness and the vehicles through which it manifests. The word "spirit" is restricted to that divinity in us that manifests on the highest planes of the universe and is distinguished by its consciousness of unity. Unity is the keynote of spirit, for below the spiritual realm all is division. When we pass from the spiritual into the intellectual, we at once find ourselves in the midst of separation.

Unity and the Spirit

Dealing with our own intellectual nature, to which the word "soul" ought to be restricted, we at once notice that it is the principle of separateness. In the growth of our intellectual nature, we become more and more conscious of the separateness of the "I." It is sometimes called the "I-ness" in us. It gives rise to all our ideas of separate existence, separate property, separate gains and losses.

74

Intellect is just as much a part of us as spirit, only a different part, and it is the very antithesis of the spiritual nature. For where the intellect sees "I" and "mine," the spirit sees unity, nonseparateness; where the intellect strives to develop itself and assert itself as separate, the spirit sees itself in all things and regards all forms as equally its own.

The great mysteries of the religions of the world all turn on the spiritual nature, for it is a mystery to the ordinary person. What Christians call the Atonement belongs entirely to the spiritual nature, and can never be understood so long as we think of ourselves as separate intellects, intelligences apart from others. For the very essence of the Atonement lies in the fact that the spiritual nature, being everywhere one, can pour itself out into one form or another. It is because this fact of the spiritual nature has not been understood, and only the separation of the intellect has been seen, that the great spiritual doctrine has been changed into the substitution of one individual for other individuals. It has not been recognized that the Atonement is wrought by the all-pervading spirit, which can pour itself into any form at will.

The spirit is that part of human nature in which the sense of unity resides, the part in which primarily we are one with God, and secondarily one with all that lives throughout the universe. A very old Upanishad begins with the statement that all this world is God-inveiled, and going on then to speak of one who knows that vast, pervading, all-embracing unity, it bursts into a cry of exultation: "What then becomes of sorrow, what then becomes of delusion, for him who has known the unity?" That sense of a oneness at the heart of things is the testimony of the spiritual consciousness, and only as that is realized is it possible that the spiritual life will manifest. The technical names do not matter at all. They are drawn from the Sanskrit, which for millennia has given definite names to every stage of human and other consciousness.

This mark of unity is the one on which we may rest as the sign of the spiritual nature. According to an old Eastern book, "the man who sees the One Self in everything, and all things in the Self, he seeth, verily, he seeth." All else is

blindness. The sense of separation, while necessary for evolution, is fundamentally a mistake. The separateness is only
like the branch that grows out of a trunk, the unity of the
life of the tree passes into every branch and makes them all a
oneness. It is the consciousness of that oneness which is the
consciousness of the spirit.

In Christianity the sense of oneness has been personified
in the Christ. The first stage—where there is still the Christ
and the Father—is where the wills are blended, "not my
will but thine be done." The second stage is where the sense
of unity is felt: "I and my Father are one." In that manifestation of the spiritual life we have the ideal which underlies
the deepest inspiration of the Christian sacred writings, and
it is only as "the Christ is born in man," to use the Christian
symbol, that the truly spiritual life begins.

This is very strongly pointed out in some of the Epistles.
St. Paul wrote to Christians and not to the profane or hea-
then. He wrote to those who had been baptized, who were
recognized members of the Church, in a day when member-
ship was more difficult to gain than it is in these later times.
Paul says to them, "Ye are not spiritual: ye are carnal." The
reason he gives for regarding them thus is, "I hear that there
be divisions among you." Where the spiritual life is dominant, harmony and not division is to be found.

The second great stage of the spiritual life is also marked
out in the Christian scriptures, as in all other great world
scriptures, when it is said that when the end comes, all that
has been gathered up in the Christ, the Son, is gathered up
yet further into the Father, and "God shall be all in all."
Even that partial separation of Son and Father vanishes,
and the unity is supreme. Whether we read the *Upanishads*,
the *Bhagavad Gita*, or the *New Testament*, we find ourselves in exactly the same atmosphere as regards the meaning and nature of the spiritual life: it is that which knows
the oneness, that in which unity is complete.

Now this is possible for us in spite of the separation of the
intellect which bars us from each other, because in the heart
of our nature we are divine. That is the great reality on
which all the beauty and power of human life depend. It is

no small thing whether a people believes they are divine or have been deluded into the idea that they are by nature sinful, miserable and degraded. Nothing is so fatal to progress, nothing so discouraging to the growth of the inner nature, as the continual repetition of that which is not true: that we are fundamentally and essentially wicked, not divine. It is a poison at the very heart of life; it stamps one with a brand which is hard indeed to throw off. If we want to give even the lowest and most degraded a sense of inner dignity, which will enable them to climb out of the mud in which they are plunged to the dignity of a divine human nature, we must tell them of their essential divinity, that in their hearts they are righteous and not foul. For it is just in proportion that we do so, that within them there will be faint stirrings of the spirit, so overlaid that they are not conscious of it in their ordinary life. If there is one duty of preachers of religion more vital than another, it is that all who hear them shall feel the stirring of the Divine within themselves.

Unfolding the Spiritual Nature

Looking thus at everyone as divine at heart, we begin to ask: if that is the meaning of spirit and spiritual life, what is the method for unfolding it? The first step, as mentioned, is to get people to believe in it, to put aside all that has been said about the human heart being "desperately wicked," about original sin. There is no original sin except ignorance, and we are all born into that. We have to grow slowly out of it by experience, which gives us wisdom. That is the starting point, as the conscious sense of unity is the crown. The method of spiritual life is whatever enables the life to show itself forth in reality, as it ever is in essence. Our inner Divinity—that is the inspiring thought we want to spread through all the churches, which too long have been clouded by a doctrine exactly the reverse. When we once believe ourselves divine, we will seek to justify our inner nature.

Now the method of the spiritual life in the fullest sense cannot, I frankly admit, be applied to the least developed among us. For them the very first lesson is that ancient one, "Cease to do evil." One of my favorite Upanishads speaks of the steps by which one may search for and find the Self, the God within. The first step, it is said, is to "cease to do evil." That is the first step towards the spiritual life, the foundation which must be laid. The second step is active: to do the right. They are no less true because they are commonplace. They are necessary everywhere and must be repeated until evil is forsaken and good embraced. The spiritual life cannot begin until one completes these steps.

Regarding the later steps, it is written that no one who is slothful, who is unintelligent, who is lacking in devotion can find the Self. And again it is said that "The Self is not found by knowledge nor by devotion, but by knowledge wedded to devotion." These are the two wings that lift us up into the spiritual world.

We may find a mass of details in the various scriptures of the world to fill in these broad outlines which guide us to the narrow ancient Path. But what is specially needed just now is a way in which people living in the world—bound by domestic ties, and occupations of every sort—may gain the spiritual life, by which they may secure progress in real spirituality.

In the different religions of the world there has been a certain inclination to draw a line of division between the life of the world and the life of the spirit. That line, which is real, is however often misunderstood and misrepresented. It is thought to consist in circumstance, whereas it consists in attitude—a profound difference, and one vitally important to us. Owing to this misunderstanding, men and women in all ages have left the world in order to find the Divine. They have gone out into desert and jungle and cave, into mountain and solitary plain, imagining that by giving up what they called "the world," the life of the spirit might be secured. And yet if God is all-pervading and everywhere, Divinity must be in the marketplace as much as in the desert, in the bank as much as in the jungle, in the court of law as much as in the solitary mountain, in human haunts as well as in lonely places. It is true that the weaker souls can more easily sense the all-pervading life away from the jangle of humanity, but that is a sign of weakness and not spirituality. It is not the strong, the heroic, the warrior, who asks for solitude in seeking the spiritual life.

Yet the solitary life has its place, and often a man or woman will go aside into some lonely place and dwell there in solitude for a lifetime. But that is never the last and crowning life; it is not the life in which the Christ walks the earth. Such a life sometimes prepares one to break off ties which one is otherwise not strong enough to break. People run away because they cannot battle; they evade what they cannot face. That is often a wise policy; and for anyone easily tempted, it is good advice to avoid temptation.

But the true heroes of the spiritual life avoid no place and no person. They are not afraid of polluting their garments, for they have woven them of stuff that cannot be soiled. Those who live the solitary life will return again to lead the life of the world. The lesson of detachment they learned in the solitary places will serve them well when they return to ordinary life. Liberation, the freeing of the spirit, that conscious life of union with God which is the mark of the human become divine, that last conquest is won in the world, not in the jungle or desert.

Renouncing the Fruit of Action

The spiritual life is gradually won, and the lessons of the spirit learned in this world—but on one condition. This condition embraces two stages: first, we do all that ought to be done because it is our duty. As the spiritual life dawns, we recognize that all our actions are to be performed, not for some particular result, but because it is our duty to perform them. This is easily said, but how hard to accomplish! We need not change anything in our life to become spiritual, but we must change our attitude to life. We must cease to ask anything from it and give everything we do to it, because it is our duty.

Now that conception of life is the first great step towards the recognition of unity. If there is only one great Life, if each of us is only an expression of that Life, then all our activity is simply the working of that Life within us, and the results are reaped by the common Life and not by the separated self. This is what is meant in the *Gita* by giving up working for fruit—for the fruit is the ordinary result of action.

This advice is only for those who will to lead the spiritual life, for it is not advisable for people to give up working for the fruit of action until a more potent motive has arisen within them, one that spurs them into activity without a prize for the personal self. We must have activity, it is the way of evolution. Without activity we do not evolve; without effort and struggle we float in the backwaters of life and make no progress along the river. Activity is the law of progress; as we exercise ourselves, new life flows into us. For that reason it is written that one who is slothful may never find the Self. Those who are slothful and inactive have not even begun to turn to the spiritual life.

The motive for action for ordinary people is quite properly the enjoyment of the fruit. This is God's way of leading the world along the path of evolution. Prizes are put before us. We strive after the prizes, and as we strive develop our powers. But when we seize the prize, it crumbles to pieces in our hands—always. If we look at human life, we see this continually repeated. You desire money; gain it, millions. In the midst of the millions a deadly discontent invades you; you become weary of the wealth that you are not able to use. You strive for fame and win it, and then you call it "a voice going by, to be lost on an endless sea." You strive for power, and when you hold it, power palls and you are weary and disappointed. The same sequence is ever repeated.

These are the toys which the Father holds out to induce his children to exert themselves. He himself hides within the toy in order to win the children; for there is no beauty and no attraction anywhere except for the life of God. But when the toy is grasped the life leaves it; it crumbles in the hand, and we are disappointed. For the value lies in the struggle and not in the possession, in putting forth powers to obtain, and not in the idleness after victory. And so we evolve, and until these delights have lost their power to attract, it is well that they continue to goad us to effort and struggle.

But when the spirit begins to stir and to seek its own manifestation, then the prizes lose their attractive power. We see duty instead of fruit as motive. And then we work for duty's sake, as part of the One Great Life, and we work with all the energy of those who work for fruit, perhaps even with more. Those who can work at some great scheme for human good and then, after years of labor, see it crumble before them, and remain content, they have gone far along the road of the spiritual life. Does this seem impossible? Not when we understand the Life, and have felt its unity; for in that consciousness no effort for human good is wasted, no good work fails. The form in which the work is embodied may crumble, but the life remains.

Such a motive may animate even those outside the spiritual life. Consider how sometimes in some great battle campaign success and failure are words that change their meaning when a vast host struggles for a single end. A small band of soldiers may be sent to achieve a hopeless, impossible task. A commanding officer may receive an order he knows is impossible to obey, perhaps taking a hillside bristling with cannon. He knows that before he can gain the top of that hill his regiment will be decimated, and if he presses on, annihilated. It does not make any difference to the loyal soldier who trusts his general and leads his men. He does not hesitate; he regards the command only as a proof of the confidence of his commander, that he is considered strong enough to fight and inevitably fail. But have they failed when the last man dies and only the corpses remain? It looks so to those who have seen only that little part of the struggle. But while they held the attention of the enemy, other movements that ensured victory went unnoticed. When a grateful nation raises the monument of thanks to those who have conquered, the names of those who have failed in order to make the victory of their comrades possible will hold a place of honor.

And so with those who are spiritual. They know the plan cannot fail. They know the combat must in the end be crowned with victory. It does not matter to those who have known the Oneness that this little part is stamped as failure.

It has made possible the victory of the great plan for human redemption, which is the real end for which they worked. They were not working to make a success here, to found some great institution there; they were working for the redemption of humanity. Though the form of their part of the work has been shattered, the life advances and succeeds.

That is what is meant by working for duty. It makes all life comparatively easy. It makes life calm, strong, impartial, and undaunted; for those who work for duty do not cling to anything they do. Once it is done they have no more concern with it. They let go of success or failure as the world counts them, for they know the Life within goes onward to its goal. This is the secret of peace in work. Those who work for success are always troubled, always anxious, always counting their forces, reckoning their chances and possibilities. But those who do not care for success but only for duty work with the strength of Divinity, and their aim is always sure.

Acting as Channels for the Divine

That is the first great step. In order to take it there is one secret we must remember: we must do everything as though the Great Power were doing it through us. That is what is called in the *Gita* "inaction in the midst of action." For those of the world who would become truly spiritual, that is the thought they must put behind all their work. What must be the motive in the heart of the lawyer or judge if they would learn the secret of the spirit in ordinary affairs of life? They must regard themselves simply as incarnations of Divine Justice. Even in the midst of law as we know it, imperfect as it is and full of wrongs, it is the Justice of God striving to make itself supreme on earth. Those who would be spiritual in the profession of the law must always have at the heart of their thought, "I am the divine hand of Justice in the world, and as that I follow law."

It is the same in all fields. Trade is one of the ways by which the world lives—a part of the Divine Activity. Those in trade must think of themselves as part of that circulating stream of life by which nations are drawn together. They

are the divine merchants in the world, and in them Divine
Activity must find hands and feet. And all who take part in
ruling and guiding the nation are also representatives of the
Divine Lawgiver, and only do their work right as they realize that they incarnate divine life in that aspect.

I know how strange this sounds when we think of political
strife and of the pettiness of politicians. But degradation
does not touch the reality of the Divine Presence, and in
every ruler, or fragment of a ruler, the Divine Lawgiver is
seeking to incarnate in order for the nation to have a noble,
happy and pure national life. If only a few in every walk of
life strove to lead the spiritual life, if, casting aside all fruits
of individual action, they thought of themselves as only incarnations of the many aspects of the Divine Activity in the
world, how beautiful and sublime would the life of the
world become!

It is the same in home life. In an old Hindu book it is said
that the Logos of the universe, God manifest, is the Great
Householder. Every husband should think of himself as in-
carnating the Divine Householder. His wife and children exist, not for his comfort or delight, but in order that he may
embody the Divine as perfect man, as husband and father.
The wife and mother should think of herself as the incarnation of the other side of Nature, the side of matter, the
nourisher, and embody Nature's ceaseless providing for all
her children's needs. As the great Father and Mother of all
protect and nourish their world, so are the parents to the
children in a home where the spiritual life is beginning to
grow. Thus might all life be made beautiful, and every man
and woman who begins to show the spiritual life becomes a
benediction in the home and in the world.

The Joy of Giving

The second great step that we may take, when duty is
done for duty's sake, adds joy to duty—the fulfillment of the
Law of Sacrifice. In this noblest view of life, we see ourselves not merely as the Divine Life in activity in the world,
but as the Divine Life that sacrifices itself that all may live.
For it is written that the dawn of the universe is an act of

sacrifice, and the support of the universe is the continual sacrifice of the all-pervading Spirit that animates the whole. When we realize that mighty sacrifice as the Life of the universe, it is a joy to throw ourselves into the sacrifice and have a share in it, however small, and to be part of the sacrificial life by which the worlds evolve. "Where, then, is sorrow, where, then, delusion, when once the One-ness has been seen?" That is the secret of the joy of those who are spiritual. Losing everything outside, they win everything within.

I have often said, and it remains true, that while the life of the form consists in taking, the life of the spirit consists in giving. It is this which made the Christ, as Spiritual Giver, declare, "It is more blessed to give than to receive." For, truly, those who know the joy of giving have no desire for the joy of receiving; they know the spring of unfailing joy that arises within the heart as the Life pours out. For if the Divine Life could flow into us and be kept within ourselves, it would become stagnant, sluggish, dead. But the life through which the Divine Life pours ceaselessly is not stagnant and does not get weary. The more it pours out the more it receives.

Let us not, then, be afraid to give. The more we give, the fuller shall be our life. Let us not be deluded by the world of separateness, where everything grows less as we give it. If I had gold, my store would lessen with every coin that I gave away, but that is not so with the things of the spirit. The more we give, the more we have; each act of giving makes us a larger reservoir. Thus we need not fear we will become empty, dry, exhausted, for all Life is behind us, and its springs are one with us. Once we know the Life is not ours, once we realize that we are part of a mighty unity, then the real joy of living comes, the true blessedness of a life that knows its own eternity. All the small pleasures of the world which once were so attractive fade away in the glory of true living, and we know the meaning of those great words: "He who loseth his life shall find it" unto life eternal.

9

Theosophy and Ethics

An address given at the Parliament of Religions, Chicago, 1893.

In the earliest stages of moral life, altruism must be the goal that we set before ourselves. We should strive to perfect the service to others. But altruism is a stage of progress rather than the goal. As long as service is done consciously as service to others who are separated from our own self, there is still some incompleteness in our ethics, some lack of spirituality in our soul.

There is an exquisite Persian poem in which the lover, seeking his beloved, finds the door of her chamber closed. He knocks, pleading for admission. From within the closed room comes a voice saying, "Who asks for admission?" Believing his love to be his best claim for entry, he answered, "It is thy beloved that knocks." But there was silence within the room and the door remained closed.

He went out into the world and learned deeper lessons of life and of love. Coming back once more to the closed door, he knocked and asked for entry. Again the voice came, "Who is it that knocks?" But the answer this time was no longer "thy beloved." "It is thyself that knocks," he said. The door opened and he passed through it.

All true love has its root in unity, where it is not two but one. So in the highest ethics this is the true note that we should strike. For our most beloved there is no such thing as service regarded as altruistic, because the deepest joy and the highest pleasure come in serving the better self of each. As we grow in spiritual life and understand the true oneness of humanity, we find the best beloved is humanity itself. We serve our higher Self in serving it, and thus we return to that from which we started, the Invisible, the One and the All.

Altruism, glorious as it is in the lower stages of morality, is lost in the Supreme Oneness of the human soul, in the absolute indivisibility of the Spirit. While we are still consciously separate, altruism may be regarded as the Law of Life, based on our common origin in the Divine. We share common training on the pilgrimage every soul must tread, common experience in learning every lesson, acquiring all knowledge, sharing the various possibilities of the human lot, and building a sublime character out of common material. Our destiny is one: the perfection of a divine humanity that is one in origin and one in training. Of what value is it to separate one person from another, to build walls of division between brothers and sisters?

Roots of Brotherhood

Unity is the foundation of our brotherhood, as "brotherhood" is the word that includes all our ethics. All true conduct has its root in the Law of Love. As long as external law is needed, that law is the measure of our imperfection. Only when no law is wanted, when the nature expressing itself spontaneously is one with the Divine Law, is humanity perfected and liberty and law become one.

The Categorical Imperative

Here again we see the sanction of right ethics, in this fact of brotherhood found everywhere in Nature. Ethical systems ask for some categorical imperative which announces what is right and what is our duty. In Immanuel Kant's system and everywhere else the same question is propounded: What is the imperative, what is the ought, what is the "thou shalt," which is to be the basis for ethical training?

Some schools hold that an imperative cannot be found, that we are face to face with a difficulty as to why we ought. Can we get any further than a conditional imperative? Can we go beyond the statement that if you want to reach a certain goal, you should pursue such-and-such a path? You may say to an art student, "If you want to paint and be a great artist, you must hold your brush in such fashion; you must train your eye by such-and-such rules; you must gradually gain the knowledge which underlies form, and by these many steps you shall at last reach your goal."

Is morality the same in this sense as art or science? Does it always depend on an "if," so that those who refuse the goal reject right conduct and stand lawless in a universe of law? If that is so, it seems to me that human progress will be very slow, for you would first have to evolve conscience, and training of the conscience is needed for right ethics. You would be walking constantly in a vicious circle with no starting point. You would be trying to use a lever with no fulcrum, and so find no point to which your force could be applied. We need the categorical imperative, not the conditional, not, "If you would be perfect, do this or that," but, "you shall be perfect, and the Law of Life is thus."

Is it not true that Nature speaks in this way? Is it not true that Nature sounds the categorical imperative? Humans, ignorant and foolish, not knowing the laws that surround them, desire to follow the promptings of their own untrained will. They are driven, perhaps, by the desires of the lower nature and hear in them the voice that allures and compels. Nature mandates sternly, "Thou shalt." The human will, able to choose, answers "I will not." Then two words fall upon the silence: "Then suffer."

Such is the way in which physical nature teaches the inviolability of law. Humans strive to follow their own untrained will. They dash themselves against the iron wall they cannot break, and the pain of the bruises teaches them that law is inviolable and unchangeable, that it must be obeyed or the disobedient will perish in the struggle.

Is Nature different on different planes? Does she speak as clearly in the moral and spiritual worlds as in the physical? All Nature is one. The expression of the one Divine Will is Nature, and until you can change the Divine Will no law that expresses that Will can be altered. Therefore, in morals as much as in physics, this categorical imperative holds.

But unhappily, it has not been undisputed; unhappily, some have thought they could play with morals where they would never dream of playing with physical necessity. They have thought that they could sow one seed and reap another, not knowing they were sowing virtue and vice instead of merely corn or oats. They have not understood that each seed is ripened after its own nature. The moral seed has ripened according to law and yielded a corrupt society, degraded humanity and souls stupefied and drugged by sense.

Does this teaching seem stern and cold? Does it seem as though we are in a remorseless universe with the wheels of destiny rolling around us and no place of refuge in which to escape? Do you feel that these wheels will crush you, that law is iron and destiny cannot be escaped? If to you law seems cruel and death soulless, you do not understand the universe.

Divine Law

Law is but the Will of the Divine, and the Divine desires your happiness. Law is but the expression of the perfect, and only in perfection can joy and peace be found. Though the wheels roll on unchanging, the very heart of the universe is love. Some of us have caught glimpses of this unity, have seen that love and justice are one, and that injustice and cruelty would be identical. Therefore looking at the universe, we sometimes feel that, while the law is changeless, it lifts us instead of crushing us.

Ralph Waldo Emerson taught the same lesson. In one of those marvelous essays of his, he taught the great truth that Nature looks cruel only while you oppose her; she is your strongest helper when you join yourself to her. For every law that crushes you while you oppose it lifts you when you are united to it. Every force that is against you while you are lawless is on your side when you make yourself one with law. Emerson tells you to hitch your wagon to a star, for then the wagon shall move with all the force of the planet above you. Is it not a greater destiny to suffer until we learn the law than to escape it and remain in ignorance, as it is the law that ultimately brings us triumph? Nature is conquered by obedience; the Divine is found in a unity of justice and love.

Brotherhood, then, in its full meaning, is a law in Nature. This cannot be stressed too much. It is the object of our work for brotherhood to become practical in society, and it will never become practical until people understand that it is a law and not only an aspiration. When we discover a law of Nature, we no longer fight against it. We at once accommodate ourselves to the new knowledge and adapt to the newly understood conditions. Yet brotherhood is so little known in our Western world! Is it possible that people have disobeyed the law, not because they do not recognize the beauty of the ideal, but because they have not understood its absolute necessity, that every effort that goes against the Universal Law in life fails?

We are brothers and sisters in our bodies by the interactions of physical molecules. We are brothers and sisters in our minds by that interaction of mental images and mental pictures with which every one of us is constantly affecting others. We are brothers and sisters in our spirits, above all. On every plane of life, brotherhood exists as fact.

Ladder of Love

The word "brotherhood" is meant to imply everything that it means in the closest relationships of daily life. We are apt to make a distinction between brothers and sisters in church and those outside. Sometimes it is said that by ceasing to love those nearest to us, we grow to love impersonal humanity. It is not so. The life of love is a growth upward, an ever-widening expansion from the family to the city, from the city to the state, from the nation to humanity. It does not begin by dwarfing love in the home. It starts there and builds on the passion and the pity that the mother feels for her child, and extends that love to embrace every child, not by cooling down love, but by strengthening and widening it.

Thus brotherhood is to grow and the race to become one practically, as it is essentially. For it is these relationships that teach the wider possibility, and so, in *The Book of the Golden Precepts*,* one of the most exquisite gifts that we have received from the East through H. P. Blavatsky, we are told, "Follow the wheel of life; follow the wheel of duty to race and kin." As those duties are properly discharged, we become worthy of the wider work. The heart widens and is never closed to anyone. At the very beginning of the path, the disciple's first step is to make his or her heart respond to every cry. As the heartstring quivers under the touch, the disciple, as string, shall quiver to every cry of need.

But if we confine our love to those near us, it is lower love. The lower love is selfish, exclusive, giving to those personally beloved, without caring for the wants of others when one's own family is satisfied. That is a form of selfishness. When you find in a teaching that such love is to be destroyed, it means that love must be purified of every taint of personality.

We must grow upward, widening as we grow. The love we are to give to brothers and sisters is to be measured by their need and not by any of the lesser ties of personality that may bind us to them or may be absent. The measure of want, that is the measure of giving. The agony that cries for help, that is the claim that we have to answer. So our teachers train us to discharge the duty at hand so that we may carry the strength of that to the wider duty. Thus we make our love to all people as the love of husband to wife, as the love of brother to sister. Any pain we find in that love is but joy in the sacrifice; the happiness of the beloved is deeper than any momentary pain it may bring.

Thus, we learn, that which Nature tells us as regards human brotherhood. From that we step onward to deal with those who are not quite yet touched with that light of

---

*H. P. Blavatsky's *The Voice of the Silence* was derived from this mystic treatise.

right livelihood, that is, right fashion of supporting ordinary life, an honest way of gaining the means of ordinary existence. This does not mean a livelihood based on being compelled to serve others, nor a livelihood which takes everything and gives nothing back, nor one which stretches out its hands to grasp and closes its fists when gift is asked instead of gain. Right livelihood implies honesty of living, and honesty implies that you give as much as you take, that you render back more than you receive, that you measure your work by your power of service, not by your power of compulsion. Right livelihood implies that the stronger your brain the greater your duty to help, the higher your position the greater the imperative to bend that position to the service of human need. Right livelihood is based on justice and is made beautiful by love.

But on the material plane more is asked than livelihood that injures none and serves all. You also have a duty of right living that touches on the plane of the body, by which I include the whole of the transitory part of our nature. Right living means recognizing the influence you bring to bear upon the world by the whole of your lower nature as well as by your higher. It implies understanding the duty that your body bears to the bodies of all, for you cannot separate your bodies from the bodies amidst which you live, since constant interchange is going on between them. Tiny lives that build up your body today help to build up another's tomorrow, and so the constant interaction and interweaving of these physical molecules proceeds.

What use do you make of your body? Do you say, "It is mine. I can do with it as I will"? But, nothing we have is our own, for all belongs to that greater ourselves, the aggregate of humanity. The fragments have no rights that go against the claim of service to the whole. So you are responsible for the use that you make of your body. If, for example, when these tiny lives come into your charge, you poison them with alcohol or render them coarse and gross with overluxurious living, you send them out to other men and women and children where they sow seeds of the vices they have learned from you. They spread the gluttony, the intemperance, the impurity of living that you have stamped on them while they remained as part of your own body. Every human being who helps to spread poison in a community is responsible for alcoholism and addiction that becomes focalized in those miserable creatures who suffer from these. You are guilty of your brother's or sister's degradation if you do not supply pure atoms of physical life to build up others, who in very truth are one with yourself.

Here you see something of what service means on this lower plane. You could set an example for another kind of service, so that others may learn from your voluntary action. You could simplify your physical life, lessen physical wants. You could think less of luxury and more of the higher life, spend less time on the artificial wants of the body and more time on helping others grow less encumbered with the anxieties of life.

You hardly dare to put a spiritual teaching to those on whom the iron yoke of poverty presses and who find in physical suffering one of the miseries of their lives. You should set the ideal of plain living and high thinking instead of the ideal of senseless luxury and gross materialistic living. Can you blame the poor for thinking so much of earthly pleasure and so passionately desiring material ease? Can you blame them if discontent grows when you set the ideal which they copy? You, by the material pleasure of your lives, tell them that the aim and object of human life is but the joy of the senses, the pleasure of the moment.

This, also, is your duty in service on the material plane. Lessening the wants of the body, you may learn to feed the soul; making your outer life more nobly simple, you may give your energies rather to that which is permanent and which endures.

Service on the Mental Plane

Not only on the physical plane, the lowest, is service to be sought. On the mental plane humanity can be served far more efficaciously than on the physical plane. Do you think that you cannot do service on the mental plane, that the mental plane is for great thinkers who publish some works that revolutionize thought? Do you think work on the mental plane is for the speaker who reaches thousands where you can reach but units? It is not so. Great thinkers, whether writers or speakers, do not have such enormous influence as you may imagine judging by outer appearances. True, their work is great, but have you ever been struck by the source of the speakers' power, the source of the strength with which they move a crowd? It does not lie in themselves, not in their own power, but in the power they are able to evoke from the men and women they address, from the human hearts they awaken. It is the energy of the audience and not the speaker in the tide of the speech. Orators are but the tongues that put into language the thoughts in the hearts of the people who are not able to articulate them. The thoughts are already there, and when some tongue puts them into speech, when other inarticulate senses take the force of the spoken word, then people think it is oratory. It is their own hearts that move them, and it is their own voice —inarticulate in the people—which makes the power that rings from land to land.

That is not all. Every one of you has thoughts that you pour out into the world by your daily thinking. You are creating the possibilities of the future and making or marring the potencies of today. Even as you think, the thought burning in your brain becomes a living force for good or evil in the mental atmosphere. The vitality and strength in it carry it on to its work of this world of mind.

There is no one, however weak, however obscure, who does not have one of the creature forces of the world in his or her soul. As we think, thoughts go out to mold the thoughts and lives of others. As we think thoughts of love and gentleness, the whole reservoir of love in the world is filled to overflowing. As we contribute to this, so we contribute to forming public opinion that molds humanity's ideas more than we dream. Everyone has a share in this. Your thought power makes you creative gods in the world, and it is thus that the future is built. It is thus that the race climbs upward to the Divine.

Constant service is to be sought not only in the physical

and mental spheres. No words or oratory can fitly describe the nature or sacredness of the service of the spiritual sphere. That is work that is done in silence, without sound of spoken word or clatter of human endeavor. That work lies above us and around us. We must have learned the perfection of service in the lower spheres before we dare aspire to climb to where the spiritual work is done.

The Power of High Ideals

What is the effect of such philosophical thought applied in the world today? Surely it is that we should think nobly, that our ideals should be lofty. In daily life we should ever strike the highest keynote, and then strive to attune our living to that keynote. Our will is lifted by the ideal. We become that which we worship.

Let us see, then, that what we worship shall have in it the power to transform us into the image of the perfect human being, into the perfect gold of which humanity shall finally consist. If you would help in that evolution and bear your share in that great labor, then let your ideal be truth, truth in every thought and act of life. Think truly; otherwise you will act falsely. Let nothing of duplicity, nothing of insincerity, nothing of falsehood soil the inner sanctuary of your life, for if that is pure your actions will be spotless, and the radiance of the eternal truth shall make your lives strong and noble.

Not only be true, but also be pure, for out of purity comes the vision of the Divine, and only the pure in heart, as said the Christ, shall see God. In whatever phrase you put it, whatever words describe it, that is true. Only the pure in heart shall have the beatific vision, for only those who are pure can share in that which is itself absolute purity.

To these ideals of truth and purity we must add one that is lacking in modern life: the ideal of reverence for what is noble, of adoration for what is higher than oneself. Modern life is becoming petty because we are not strong enough for reverence. It is becoming base, sordid and vulgar because people fear that they will sink if they bow to that which is greater than themselves. But worship of that which is higher than yourself raises you; it does not degrade you. The feeling of reverence is a feeling that lifts you up; it does not take you down. We have talked so much about rights that we have forgotten that which is greater than our rights. It is the power of seeing what is nobler than we have dreamed and bowing before it till it permeates our life and makes us like itself. Only those who are weak are afraid to obey; only those who are feeble are afraid of humility.

With the world as it is today, democracy in the external world is the best way of carrying on outer life. But if it were possible that, as in ancient Egypt and India, the very gods themselves wandered the earth as humans and taught people the higher truth, trained them in the higher life, conveyed the higher knowledge, would we claim that we were their equals? Would we be degraded by sitting at their feet to learn?

If you could weave into modern life that feeling of reverence for that which is purest, noblest, grandest—for wisdom, for strength, for purity—till the passion of your reverence brings those qualities into your own life, then your future as a nation would be secure. Your future as a people would be glorious. You men and women of America, creators of the future, will you not rise to the divine possibilities which every one of you has hidden in your own heart? Why go only to the lower when the stars are above you? Why go only to the dust when the sun sends down beams on which you may rise to its very heart?

Yours is the future, for you are making it today. As you build the temple of your nation, as you hope that in the days to come it shall rise nobly among the peoples of the earth and stand as pioneer of true life, of true greatness, lay the foundations strong today. No building can stand whose foundations are rotten, no nation can endure whose foundations are not divine. You have the power; yours is the choice. As you exercise it the America of centuries to come will bless you for the way you live or condemn you for your failure; for you are the creators of the world, and as you will so it shall be.

11

The Use of Evil

The mystery of evil is a problem which has challenged the human intellect for thousands and thousands of years. It is still discussed with as much energy, eagerness and interest as if it had never been considered before. This shows that it still remains unsolved. We seem instinctively to imagine that this problem could teach valuable and important lessons if we could understand it, and that behind the mystery of evil there is hidden some priceless truth.

I do not pretend that I will solve this immemorial problem, but I hope to lay out certain considerations which may throw light upon it if you think about them. To help you carry them more easily in your minds, I have divided the subject under four heads:

1. the origin of evil
2. the relativity of evil
3. the use of evil
4. the ending of evil

I hope to show under these heads that evil is a necessary condition of manifestation and originates with manifestation. Also, I want to show that evil does not exist absolutely, in and by itself, but is relative. It exists in the relations between things and not in the things themselves, and it varies with time, with succession of events, and with the progress of the universe.

Then I hope to show the purposes evil serves, the uses it fulfills, and how we may escape from it and, through the use of evil, break the bonds that tie us to the wheel of birth and death. Although living in the world, we may live in it without generating karma, and so, to use a well-known phrase, may burn up karma in the fire of knowledge. I hope that you will work on these ideas for yourself.

The Opposites

Now let us consider the origin of evil. Realize, to begin with, that no universe can come into manifestation at all, no manifestation can occur, no multiplicity can become, no diversity can appear, unless there is limitation. The One Existence, spoken of sometimes as Brahman, is absolute and undivided; it has no attributes, no qualities. There is only unity, no diversity or multiplicity. It is "the One without a second."

When you try to think of this Existence, in the very thinking you must separate yourself from it. You as a mind endeavor to consider something which is thought of and is not the thinker. By that very effort of thought you introduce duality into that which you are trying to realize as unity. When there is separation between the thinker and thought, which is implied in the effort, there is diversity—not Brahman as One in whom there is no duality, no separated Being, in whom there is neither thinker nor thought.

Thought implies perception and an object of perception, but Brahman is absolute unity, absolute identity. We speak of thought where thought cannot exist. Brahman is unconditioned, therefore unintelligible and without limitation. Therefore, it is truly written, *That* is neither conscious nor unconscious. However, there is some deeper essence which becomes consciousness when conditioned, because consciousness implies duality, something which is conscious, and something of which it is conscious. Duality is implied the very moment the word "consciousness" is used. So in that absolute unity, where there is identity and not diversity, where there is but the secondless *One*, there is no possibility of thinking, because there is absence of conditions and limitation.

But the very moment the universe comes into being, as it were, then there must be conditions and limitation. Limitation is a condition of manifestation, for the very moment you arrive at the point of manifestation, a circumference must be drawn from the central point, the circle of a universe. Without that, thought is lost in the absolute Oneness, the identity. Within that circle thought may be exercised; the very word "manifestation" implies this limitation. Manifestation, by law of mind, at once implies its antithesis, the absence of manifestation. With anything you may think of comes its opposite, for the opposite is implied in the very act of defining: "A" implies "not-A." Therefore, we are compelled to formulate "absence of manifestation," and yet we cannot truly be said to think it.

Only by a process of limitation can a universe come into being. Conditions self-imposed within the Infinite Oneness can be recognized as the boundary that limits thought. When that is understood, the next step is very simple. Having diversity, having limitation, imperfection is at once implied. The perfect is unlimited, the limited imperfect. So imperfection must be the result of limitation. In the totality you may find perfection; it is in the whole, but not in the parts. The very moment you have parts, multiplicity, various bodies, each body considered separately is imperfect because it is less than the whole. The very fact of being a part proves that it is imperfect. A fragment cannot be perfect; only the whole can have perfection predicated of it. The existence of the universe, by the very fact of limitation, implies imperfection in the limited; every object being necessarily limited, is also necessarily imperfect, being less than the whole.

Now when you realize that, you have your origin of imperfection, of what is called evil. Thus imperfection is coeternal with the universe. Since it is limited, imperfection is a necessary condition, so that whenever a universe comes into existence, imperfection must come into existence at the same time. The fact of manifestation is the origin of imperfection.

But when we go on to deal with what is called evil, we find something more in our thoughts than this necessary imperfection of separated bodies. Although the essence of imperfection is in the very existence of the universe, that which we call evil lies in the degree of imperfection and in its relation to the rest. The very words "good" and "evil" imply relativity, the pairs of opposites necessary to thought. The word "good" is not fairly predicated of anything until the idea of evil is recognized, the "not-good"; for good and evil are correlative terms. The one can be distinguished only as being the opposite of the other, which is implicitly present in the mind at the same time.

It is a fundamental law of mind that thought must work by differences, by discriminating the difference between "A" and "not-A," "A" representing the individual thing which is thought of, and "not-A" everything else which is excluded from that individual thing. So if you say "good" you separate the good from that from which it is distinguished, the "not-good." Without this separation no idea of good can be present in the mind, for we realize "good" only by contrast with that which is "not-good" and which is distinguished from it. In the absence of that distinction there would be nothing which we could call "good." "Good" and "not-good," then, are a pair of opposites, and one is only possible by the existence of the other.

Similarly you may take another pair of opposites. Compare light with darkness. Light would have no meaning in thought if it were not for darkness or no-light. Light is only cognizable by thought because of no-light. Light-giving bodies can be recognized in thought, because all bodies do not give light; this is so much the case that the presence of non-light-giving bodies is necessary for realization of light. Astronomers tell us, startling as it seems, that the depths of space are dark, not light, although they are full of the frequencies which on the earth we recognize as light. Why? Because there are vast spaces of the mighty universe where there are no light-reflecting bodies. In the absence of these dark bodies, light cannot be thrown back and reflected. Hence space, which is full of the vibrations, is absolutely dark.

The Relativity of Evil

Take still further an extension of the same thought. Evil does not exist in and by itself, as we may judge from the phenomena around us. Evil, like good, lies in the relationship between one thing and another; it is relative, not absolute. What we speak of as evil in one place may be not evil in another. Evolution implies changing character, and what is good at one stage may be evil at another.

An illustration will show what I mean. You may have a violently vibrating body, vibrating without touching any other body. It may be vibrating inwards and outwards, which would do no harm, and not result in anything you would recognize as evil. But place another body in contact with that violently vibrating body. It will produce what we call pleasure or pain if the second body has the power of response, of answering to that which is outside and of feeling the vibration to which it answers. By coming into contact with the body which is violently vibrating, and by receiving the blow, what we call the sensation of pain might arise.

Now pain is regarded as part of the evil of the universe, as the results of what is called evil. But actually pain is the result of contact between two things which separately are innocuous. It arises from the interrelation of things which in their separate aspects are not pain-producing but only imperfect. But when coming into relation with each other, they, as it were, work against each other. What we regard as evil comes out. The nature of the result depends upon the relation between the two. It does not depend upon the inherent imperfections of each but on their relation to each other.

Now as evolution proceeds, that which we call evil must necessarily be developed more and more. The result of evolution is to bring into conscious existence higher and higher types of organisms, of living things, which enter into more and more complicated relationships with others which surround them. More and more of this power of response is developed in these organisms. Also, the memory of response is developed and the power of placing things side by side, of comparison, and of considering the results of the comparison and drawing volitions from it.

Then there is the experience, gradually gathered, which illumines the developing consciousness and enables it to recognize certain things as against progress, against higher evolution, certain things which retard evolution, and tend to bring about disintegration instead of higher integration.

Now what does evolution mean? It is merely the building together of higher and more complicated organisms that express with ever greater perfection the Life that is divine, the Life that is seeking manifestation in the universe. When we speak of manifestations as higher or lower, we really mean they express more or less of the divine. We call them higher and lower merely as they manifest qualities which tend towards the lessening of separateness or the developing of unity, which lead away from the pole of matter and toward the pole of Spirit. The grosser side of the manifestations of the One Life is what we describe as matter.

Now this implies that there are two poles in manifestation: the form side or matter on the one hand, and the life side or Spirit on the other. They are the two opposite aspects of the one Eternal Life. The process of evolution consists in that Life in its dual aspects going outwards to cause diversity and, when the limit of diversity is reached, drawing inwards to reintegrate the diverse, separate units into a mighty and enriched unity. The outward-going Life seeks diversity and may be said therefore to tend to the pole of matter. The inward-going Life seeks unity, and may be said therefore to tend to the pole of Spirit.

Here is a truth for the thoughtful to ponder. If we take good to mean all that is working in harmony with the great Law, and evil to mean all that is working against it, then qualities now regarded, and rightly regarded, as evil—selfishness, desire for material gain, etc.—would have been good during the "descent into matter," as only by these could diversity be obtained. Now they are evil, retarding the process of integration, checking the inward-flowing tide of life towards the pole of Spirit. Thus again we realize the relativity of evil, and understand that a quality which at one time was good, subserving the progress of the universe, becomes evil when it should have been left behind in the sweep of evolution. When persisting into a stage higher than that to which it belonged, it retards the progress which once it accelerated.

Evolution, on its returning path, is unfolding the life-side of nature. It is making matter more and more plastic, as it were, more and more delicate, more and more complicated in its organization. By its very complexity its equilibrium becomes so unstable that it easily takes shapes of various kinds under impulses from within; it becomes a mere graceful garment in which Life is expressed. Finally, matter is nothing more than the subtle form which expresses Life by limiting it. It changes form with every impulse from the Life, and takes on new shapes with the different impulses of the outgoing and incoming Life. This is evolution.

When we begin to understand what evolution means, we regard everything which helps towards evolution as in harmony with the purposes of the universe and, therefore, on the side of greater and greater integration, of the building of a complicated unity. Then we name "good" all that works in that direction and "evil" all the tendencies which persist from the stage of evolution in which greater diversity was sought. Realizing that evolution is now the process of building separated objects into a perfect unity, we call "good" everything which tends directly toward harmony, toward aggregation, toward unfolding higher unity, toward the expression of the divine Life with ever increasing perfection. We call "evil" everything which checks that aggregation and introduces the earlier forms into the present, everything that retards passing on to what is relatively perfect and higher.

Now suppose we carried that thought out. What would we find? We should find that what in the past caused evolution, and was not evil, becomes evil when it persists in the evolution of the higher organism, and so retards its growth. For instance, in the mineral kingdom you have minerals and stones hurled about by volcanic eruption. That eruption shivers certain bodies. Its tremendous evolution of gases, accompanied by explosions followed by the rebound of the separate materials, makes a desert of a fertile plain. You think this is evil. Yet wiser minds regard it as part of the regenerative processes of nature by which, by disintegration and collision, new combinations are rendered possible. The face of the earth is changed: mountain ranges are thrown up, rivers and channels are created and, by means of this violent destructive agency, new continents are built. Homes for higher forms of life are rendered possible in the course of evolution.

Let us pause for a moment and contemplate the way in which a continent is built. Let us watch the tremendous action of those volcanic forces and see a mountain range flung up at one place. Then let us watch the formation of mighty glaciers, great masses of ice, and see them presently begin to grind their way down the mountainside into the plain below. We see their resistless course plowing out their way, and listen as they move on, smashing, grinding, shivering, tossing up masses which fall again rebounding. We watch the processes of that world of struggle and strife, noise, disturbance and difficulty, and see the marshalling of those energies which seem to be working only for ruin.

But as centuries go on, and still you are watching, you find that where there was a grinding glacier there is now a new channel which has been dug out of the mountainside and through the plains by the glacier's action. As you watch you find water collecting in this channel and gradually more and more flowing into it until, where there was the destructive action of the ice, there is a great river full of life-giving water. As the water flows down through the plain, vegetation springs up on the banks. Great cities are built, food can be grown, trees grow luxuriantly, and homes are seen.

What would have been humanity's lot without that previous evolution? We can see that unless the disturbing agency had had full sway in earlier times, all this could not have happened. You cannot call that evil.

There is nothing evil in itself, only simple destructive and attractive forces at work. The Being who is the source of all life, the great One, the Lord, is known sometimes as the Destroyer and sometimes as the Regenerator, for until the lower is destroyed the higher cannot be born, and every death is but the lower aspect of a higher birth.

Let us turn to humanity, to those who have been gradually evolving and have begun to reason and remember, to compare, and therefore to judge and to understand. Human beings, having evolved to a stage at which the infliction of pain on others is against their evolution towards the divine love, call infliction of pain a crime. We call murder an evil act because the murderer is reverting to a previous stage in evolution that ought to have been outgrown. As a human being he or she should have evolved towards a higher life of harmony. But the murderer is giving way to an inclination which will retard growth and at this stage is harmful. At the point of evolution they should have reached, such people ought to be one of the forces evolving towards the divine harmony and not retarding evolution and rendering it slower.

The Need for Opposition

I am going to explain the use of this retarding agency. Let us suppose you begin to understand that in the sphere of thought and action you can place yourself either upon the side of progress or upon the side of retardation. You realize your place in the universe and the true working of Nature. You may deliberately set yourself either on the side of the evolving life or on the side of the forces which are retarding evolution and holding it back, which are against progress.

You have to choose with which side to identify. The choice is in your own hands. You must realize that if you choose the side which retards evolution you have chosen destruction, by identifying with the disintegrating agency. If you choose harmony with evolving life, you have chosen continuation, because you have identified with that which is the law of progress, and your identification with that law will give to you the permanence which results from harmony.

You may ask why identification with the retarding forces leads to destruction. The answer is that the Divine Life, going on and causing evolution, returns to unity; everything which harmonizes with its mighty course is carried onwards without waste of energy. On the other hand, everything which sets itself against evolution and causes friction and retardation wears itself out by the very friction it causes. It is a law of motion that a moving body continues to move if not opposed, but if friction is generated by its coming into contact with another body, it will gradually come to a standstill. Wherever there is friction there is expenditure of energy; friction transmutes the energy of motion into another form such as heat, and the energy is dissipated. Thus, continued friction causes the dissipation of the form which is subject to it. It is not that the energy is annihilated or destroyed; that cannot be. It is that the form, which comes into contact with that in which the opposite force is manifested, is destroyed. The form perishes because the opposition breaks it into pieces, or rather it breaks itself into pieces against the opposing force. But the energy persists because it is part of One Eternal Life.

You may ask: Why this retarding force? Why should there be in evolution this action of retardation? Why should there be something which opposes? If everything is from the One, how can it develop?

First, the condition of any diversity is the manifestation of the opposing poles of Spirit and matter, of light and darkness. Second, for their development it is necessary for positive qualities to be exercised against opposition. Without opposition no development is possible; without opposition no growth is possible. All growth and development result from the exercise of energy against something which opposes.

Think for a moment and you will see how true this statement is. If you want to develop strength in your muscles, how are you to do it? By exercising them, by stimulating them, not by keeping them still. There are some people who practice a particular form of asceticism, extending the arm and keeping it rigid, so that muscular contraction cannot take place. After a time the arm becomes fixed in that position; it becomes rigid. The muscles lose the power of contraction and are no longer the channels of living energy. There is stagnation, absence of effort, of pulling against resistant forces. The result is to throw the arm back, as it were, into a lower form of life, to which motion does not belong, and the arm becomes as rigid as a stone or a piece of wood. It has lost the muscular power for want of exercise, because it has remained quiet and stagnant.

If you want to develop your muscles what do you do? You lift weights. You set muscles against the weight and pull against it, putting the muscle against the opposing force in the weight. The weight tries to drag you down while you try to drag it up. The effect of this conflict is the development of muscular energy, of force in the muscle. Muscularity is developed by working against the opposing weight until it becomes stronger and able to overcome opposing forces. The more the muscle is exercised, the more powerful it becomes. This development arises entirely because it has been used in opposing weight, and by exercise has overcome the opposition. From this it has gathered life and strength, for as the muscle increases its capacity for holding life, life flows into it. The strength we can draw from the surrounding divine Life is limited only by our capacity to receive and hold.

Virtue and Evil

That is the way to use evil. The life that is in you cannot manifest its higher capacities unless you are placed under conditions in which you can develop yourselves by struggling against opposition. Evil is, as it were, the weight opposing the muscle; as you develop the body by struggling against opposing external weight, so you develop moral character by struggling against evil, which is the opposite of every virtue.

Every virtue has its opposite evil: truth and falsehood, courage and cowardice, compassion and hatred, humility and pride. All these are pairs of opposites. How can you develop truth except by struggling against the false and realizing that in the world around you there is falsehood on every side? What can you do when you realize the force of this except contradict it and place yourself in opposition to it? You will never let a false word escape your lips; never let a false thought find habitation in your brain; never let a false action disfigure your conduct. The result of the recognition of falsehood will be to develop in you the necessary power for truth. As you struggle against the tendency to falseness, you develop increasing power to be true.

Now what is Truth? Truth is Brahman; Truth is Life; Truth is the essence of what we call the Divine Life. We reach it by struggling against falsehood, developing, as it were, the virtue which is the receptacle of the Divine Life. As you enlarge and increase your capacity for Truth by struggling against falsehood—as the muscle grows larger by practicing against the weight—you are making your character a receptacle for the Divine Life, that Divine Life which shall flow into you in ever-increasing volume and give you greater power. Thus you are developing those qualities of Truth which you could never have evolved without opposition, and which, in proportion to the energies evolved by your efforts against falsehood, will purify your nature from falsity, and render true the life which you are developing.

So also with every other virtue. Courage is developed in the presence, not in the absence, of something you fear. If there were no objects which gave rise to the sensation of fear, then courage could never be evolved. But the presence of that which gives the sensation of fear increases the experience of the soul and gradually evolves courage.

Have you ever noticed in an infant that an object that was terrifying when first seen gradually loses its terrifying quality as it becomes more and more familiar? See how timid little children are; see how they see even in a strange face an object which frightens them. How shall children lose that timidity and become brave around people? Not by shutting them up in a room where they will never see anybody. If they do not see strange faces, they have no fear. Fear is generated by letting them face unknown objects. Presently they begin to understand, until out of constant experiences fear is eliminated and strength and courage take its place.

I might take virtue after virtue to show that they grow only in the face of opposition, that in the result of these opposing forces lies the value of this retarding energy. *There* is the value of the evolution of evil. It acts as a weight against the effort towards perfection and thereby develops the strength which checks the desire for these forms which are doomed to destruction. Those who choose to ally themselves with that which is doomed to destruction must share the fate of those forms they have selected for their own. But the energy which is necessary for evolution towards the condition of perfection would be absent without evil. The presence of evil in the universe makes it possible for good to grow and for perfection to triumph.

Another fundamental use of evil is the evolution of the power to discriminate between good and evil, and thus of volition, of choice. How should we distinguish Truth except by discerning it as different from that which is not true? How should we learn its value if we did not find from experience the destructive effects of falsehood, in individuals and in society? "A" is only brought into consciousness by the presence of "not-A"; the latter is necessary to the definition of the former. So our minds would remain a blank as regards Truth—we could not realize it, cognize it, define it, except by distinguishing it by its differences from not-Truth. And so with each virtue, with good in its totality. Only by recognition of evil can we know good, and experience of evil is necessary to recognize evil.

The Place of Pain

Evil is also useful as a scourge that drives us to good. For as evil is discordance with the evolving forces of the Divine Life in manifestation, it must result in pain. Pain verily *is* discordant vibration. Therefore evil inevitably brings suffering as a result, not by an arbitrary penalty but by an inherent necessity. And suffering gives rise to a feeling of repulsion towards the cause of suffering. It drives us away from the side of nature which inharmoniously and tumultuously is plunging into disintegration and carrying with it the personalities who elect to identify themselves with that.

In the mighty stream of Divine Life that circles as a universe, all are carried along. But one current whirls downwards all monstrous and disorderly growths, that they may be disintegrated into the rough materials for a new building. The other current carries onwards all who are molding themselves into orderly expressions, and who, by making themselves vehicles of the Law, share its permanence as an essential manifestation of the One Reality.

I said, when dealing with pain, that I would show you

how it is possible that this evil we see around us and recognize as evil might gradually lose its retarding power over us as the god in us evolves outwardly and fills us with strength. The line along which I have been leading you will enable you to look with understanding and, therefore, with absolute charity on all the forms of evil which surround you. You will see in them inevitable imperfections. If you see a human soul struggling in corruption and in evil, you will not feel anger nor intolerance nor hatred. You will know that this soul, just because of the evil with which it is struggling, will gradually gain strength and become triumphant over it.

At last you will understand how the Divine is in everything, in good as in evil, that Sri Krishna is the vice of the gambler as well as the purity of the righteous. Our universe will become full of hope; for you will recognize that the whole is working towards perfection and that good and evil are the two forces which cooperate to liberate the soul, the one by drawing it upwards, the other by shattering everything to which it clings and which is not God.

The point to which I wish to lead you is where, as you gradually recognize these facts, you will see that the aim of the individual self is to become perfectly at one with the inward-going stream of Divine Life. This is the beginning of understanding, the beginning of the realization of the meaning of the universe. You will begin to utilize what seems to be evil in order that you may get rid of everything which binds you to the transitory side of nature. So you will take pain as a real helper.

Pain is said to be an evil. Pain is not pleasant, but it is not an evil. It is desirable and not undesirable, for it is a condition of gaining perfection, and without it perfection cannot be. Why? Because development must become conscious; that is, there must be a gradual development of thought within us. But by what process can this be secured? When we go outward towards an object which attracts us, we at first seek only satisfaction. But there is no permanent satisfaction in the external; there is nothing that can give permanent satisfaction in the external which attracts the deluded soul.

The soul has been compared to a charioteer, standing in the chariot of the body, and using the mind as the reins to curb the horses of the senses. When the galloping horses of the senses carry the soul away to the objects of desire, how shall the soul learn that these objects are not truly desirable? How shall it lose the desire which goes out to these things which can never satisfy? And how shall it learn to turn inward to the center and seek for Brahman alone?

The soul can be led to turn towards its desires only when it finds that everything which is not Brahman passes away and in the passing gives pain. You desire the gratification of the senses. That desire can be eliminated only by discovering that sensual pleasure is very transitory, that if it is followed too far it brings about disgust and suffering and pain, and that therefore freedom and wisdom lie in getting rid of the desire for sense pleasures. If, having been attracted by the sensation of taste because it is pleasant, we find that to gratify it to the utmost brings disgust, then we begin to see that it is wiser to choose something with more permanence than the gratification of taste. The root of desire is pulled up and can no longer send out lower shoots.

You can never convince people that this is so unless they have followed the objects of the lower desires and found the results which flow from them. Argument or reasoning would not do it. But when they have gratified their taste to the full and become gluttonous, presently they will find that they have made their bodies miserable. Their lives are one long suffering. Diseases result from the gratification they have experienced, and the gratification brings pain as a result. Then they will no longer desire to gratify themselves in that way, and they will have begun the long process of cutting away the root of desire.

That is the only way desire can be finally extirpated. You can only get rid of it by gradually realizing through experience that gratification of all desire which is not going upwards is a womb of pain. Nothing but this experience can get rid of desire. The destruction of desire takes place, not by outward compulsion, but inward will, and this is wrought by pain. Hence pain, miscalled an evil, is one of the greatest blessings in order to turn us from the transitory and fix us upon the eternal. For only by pain can we possibly learn; only out of disgust with the world will arise those inward aspirations which shall at last be gratified in the vision of Truth Divine.

Misunderstanding on this matter is very easy but dangerous. The stage of the full gratification of desire that I described is the stage of the soul's childhood. It is a stage before the memory of past suffering following on gratification translates itself as the voice of conscience and warns the lower nature of the peril of yielding to desire. Once there has been sufficient experience to bring about such warning from the soul, then it is madness to disregard it and gratify desire.

Full gratification of desire belongs to the stage where one yields to outer attraction without a pause or doubt, without a question. It is followed by no regret, no shame or remorse. Any question as to the propriety or wisdom of gratifying the desire shows that the memory of the soul contains a record of suffering that followed on similar gratification in the past; otherwise no question could arise. If one yields against the warning, the pain of remorse will be added to the pain of satiety.

Thus progressive lessons are learned, until at last we realize that wisdom lies in refusing to purchase future pain by temporary pleasure. And then we begin to starve out the desires by refusing to feed them. By dwelling on the pains that gratification brings, we cut at their root with the axe of knowledge, wrought out of experience.

All average people, all but the lowest and most brutish, have reached the stage where the voice of conscience is heard. They should therefore begin consciously to cooperate with the upward tendency that draws them out of the mire of materiality into the spiritual life.

Action without Desire

But how can we break our bonds? The real answer is suggested in that law I have been showing to you. The bonds are broken by these inevitable experiences which life after life teach the soul the nature of the universe into which it has come. But desire is a binding force, and as long as there is desire, so long must we come back to birth. We will be drawn back by the desire for good as well as the desire for evil; the desire for religious happiness as well as the desire for earthly joys; the desire for praise, for love, for knowledge even. A soul may desire results of a high and noble character. Still there is a desire for results, and this binds one to places where the results are to be found.

Therefore in order to get rid of karma we must get rid of *desire*. We need not cease from action, but we must act without desire—making every necessary effort, yet being indifferent to the result. This is the familiar lesson given by Sri Krishna; this the essence of all truth. It is renunciation of desire, not of action, which makes the real sannyasi, the renunciator, a *real* yogi—not simply one who is an outward renunciator in the wearing of yellow garments and ashes, but one who has broken all the bonds of desire. For those people of action who perform every action because it is their duty and remain indifferent to the fruits thereof, such ones in the world are the servants of God. They perform every action, not for what it brings them, but because it fills something lacking in the world.

Such wise ones realize that the wheel of life must turn, and they take part in the turning, not for what it may bring to them, but in order that the Divine Life may circle in its course. They play their part in working without attachment, without desire, and turn the wheel, whether it brings them pleasure or pain, praise or blame, fame or ignominy, divine knowledge or ignorance. They perceive only that it is their duty to cooperate with God while manifestation persists. They therefore identify themselves with the God from whom the turning of the wheel proceeds.

Such a person is then *one* with Sri Krishna who declared that he had nothing to obtain in heavens or on earth, but that if he stopped acting all would stop. Therefore devotees who act, not in order to get anything but in order that the divine purpose may be fulfilled, work by way of sacrifice. They offer all actions as sacrifices to God and remain indifferent to the fruits of the sacrifice, for the fruits lie at the feet of God and not in the heart of the devotee.

Such yogis make no karma, for they have no desire; they create no links which bind them to earth. They are spiritually free, although actions may spring up around them on every side. Thus is it when one is born into the sphere of knowledge; thus is it when one is born into the sphere of devotion. The life of such a person is as an altar, and burning upon that altar is the flame of devotion and of knowledge. Every action is cast into the fire and is consumed by it, rising up as the smoke of a sacrifice, and leaving behind on the altar nothing but the fuel of knowledge and the fire of love.

Such then imperfectly sketched—for the subject is vast— are the lines along which you may study the ancient problem. These hints may make more clear to you the reason pain and imperfection exist. We have seen that evil originates in limitation. We have seen that evil is but a relative thing, and how what we call evil is often only a veil over a future good. We have seen how some actions by developed humans become evil, though in a lower organism they would not be evil at all; how as we proceed onward, we can use evil for our own perfecting; how we try to escape from pain and pursue pleasure; how desire remains in our hearts, and brings us back to earth; and we go forward purifying desire, identifying ourselves with the Divine Actor in the universe. We have seen that then no further actions have binding force upon us. We become free from evil and free from all those bonds which tie our souls, until finally we become an altar from which the smoke of sacrifice goes up continually to the Eternal.

This is indeed the only life worth living, the road along which lies peace. It is realized only by the true yogi. Compare this life with that of one who clings to the world, full of dissatisfaction, full of discontent. Look at the men and women around you. Look at their faces. See how they are full of anxiety and desire, of trouble and injustice. See how their hearts are pierced by pain and laid desolate by catastrophes, by miseries, by hopes and by fears, how they are tossed about and flung from side to side, and too often brought to ruin.

Then realize that Brahman is bliss. How? Bliss because there is unity, because there is absence of desire, bliss because there is knowledge of permanence which nothing transient can disturb. So shall the despairing human soul find hope, find peace, if it is fixed on Brahman. Who can deny hope and peace to the soul that knows its source, that has found the Self? Thou art Brahman. There is nothing which can shake that, nothing which can undo or change it. It is fixed indissolubly upon the changeless, upon the Eternal Truth. It has nothing in it of earth, that it should ever pass away.

The body is not the soul. Disease may mar the body, accident may injure it, death may strike it away. But the soul remains unchanged. You may destroy the lower mind, but there is no real loss; individual circumstances may be changed, but the "I" is changeless. Separation between bodies may come, but the inner unity remains unbroken. Any outer change cannot drive such a soul to misery or despair. It stands as a rock in the midst of surging billows. The waves of misfortune boil up around it; they may dash against it, but only to be shattered into foam against its sides, and fall in snowy wreaths to decorate its base and thus render it more beautiful.

So is it with the soul which identifies itself with the One. So is it with the soul which by knowledge and devotion has removed everything which is fleeting and has founded itself on that which is divine. That is the goal, a goal which may be reached by all by the use of evil in the universe.

12

The Quest for God

Humankind has for ages fashioned theories about God, theories ranging from the fetish of tribal cultures to the loftiest dream of the mystic and the profoundest conception of the philosopher. Omitting fetishism, we may class the theories of living interest under monotheism and pantheism, including under the first the theism of modern religion and under the latter the polytheism of the great Eastern religions.

In the West many of the more thoughtful and highly educated people—repelled by the crude theism and unintelligent theories of the divine existence presented by popular Christianity—have taken refuge in agnosticism, a confession of intellectual despair. Feeling that knowledge about God is unattainable, that "no thoroughfare" is written above every path along which humanity gropes after God, these people—truthful and sincere, thoughtful and candid—have preferred the modesty of silence to the insolence of disbelief. They elected to starve the heart rather than to stifle the intellect, and consoled themselves with the undeniable facts of this world rather than what they considered as the unverifiable fancies about another. But the ineradicable longings of the human heart for the knowledge of God will sooner or later overthrow any edifice of agnosticism that the intellect can rear. Agnosticism can never be more than the temporary refuge of the wearied intellect, where it may gather strength and courage to start on another stage of the eternal quest.

Christian Concepts of God

The popular Christian conceptions of God are dominated by ideas inherited from exoteric Hebraism, by the crude anthropomorphism of its published scriptures. Jehovah, or Yahveh, of the Hebrews is imaged as a "man of war" with human passions and superhuman powers, walking in the garden, coming down from heaven to look at a tower, descending to a mountain to proclaim his law, demanding the slaughter of countless animals in sacrifice, declaring himself to be jealous, angry, revengeful, remembering offenses generation after generation. This deity of an undeveloped race has been largely instrumental in forming the God-idea of the uneducated in Christendom.

The contact of the Hebrews with Chaldean thought added dignity and grandeur to their idea of God, and their post-Babylonian writings show a nobler view of the Divine Being. The God of the prophets, as of the later Isaiah and of Micah, is a grand and inspiring conception, a Power that makes for righteousness.

This remodeled thought about God was softened into the ideal of a perfect man of superhuman greatness, the Father and Lover of humanity, in the later rabbinical teachings and in the Jewish-Christian scriptures. The limitations were removed while the ideal humanity was left; power remained without cruelty and justice without severity. But in Christian theology, such as we find in Tertullian and less nakedly in other Fathers of the Church, the savagery of the earlier Hebrews reappears and the gracious lineaments of "the Father" vanish under the fierce mask of Yahveh, again the vengeful God whelming his foes under fire-floods.

Nonetheless, the nobler conception remained as an encouragement and inspiration, gradually becoming focused in the person of the Son, the divine man, supreme in tenderness and compassion. From the troublous times of the fourth, fifth, and sixth centuries, enough emerged to satisfy the heart, but not enough to content the intellect. The conception of God was left vague, hazy, and somewhat terrifying, while the object presented for adoration, on which all love was lavished, was the Son, self-sacrificed, redeeming, surrendering power to pity—a figure that drew all hearts, that satisfied all aspirations, the man divine enough for worship, the God human enough for love.

Theism

In what we might call modern theism, which arose from the Unitarian school of Christianity, a vast superhuman personal God is regarded as at once the Father of spirits and the all-sustaining, self-existent Life, embracing and pervading all, beyond whom nothing exists. He is at once the "One without a second" and the personal lover and friend of humanity. If all the harsher traits were expunged from the God of Muhammad and the fierce wrath were replaced with an immeasurable compassion, then, for the unity and personality of the Supreme, theism and Islam might link hands.

Theodore Parker, Unitarian minister and a leader of the Transcendental movement, said: "The mode of man's finite being is of necessity a receiving: of God's infinite being, of necessity a giving. You cannot conceive of any finite thing existing without God, the infinite ground and basis thereof; nor of God existing without something. God is the necessary logical condition of a world, its necessitating cause; a world, the necessary logical condition of God, His necessitated consequence. . . . It is the idea of God as infinite—perfectly powerful, wise, just, loving, holy—absolute being, with no limitation. . . . His Here conterminous with the all of space, His Now coeval with the all of time." (*Ten Sermons on Religion*, pp. 338, 339, 341.)

"The soul contemplates God as a being who unites all these various modes of action, as manifested in truth, in right, and in love. It apprehends him, not merely as absolute truth, absolute right, and absolute love alone, but as all these unified into one complete and perfect being, the Infinite God. He is the absolute object of the soul, and corresponds thereto, as truth to the mind, as justice to the conscience, as love to the heart." (*Ibid*, p. 9.)

Science and Religion

As intellect developed and knowledge increased, science began to undermine the popular theory about God, and to see inconsistencies in the loftier thought. The universe widened with the opening of immeasurable depths of space. We caught glimpses of far suns which dwarf our own to rushlight; whirling infinities of innumerable systems; gold-dust sprinkled afar that was found to be galaxies of stars— each star a sun; faint mist-wreaths that turned out to be un-counted hordes of luminaries on the edges of new fields of being. The unplumbed profundities of living things appeared in ever-diminishing minuteness, too small for scanning; infinities, on the other hand, were found that are too vast for measuring. From all this the brain staggered back, dizzied and confounded, overturning the idol of an extra-cosmic God. Void pealed back to void, orb tossed back to orb the mournful cry, "Children, you have no Father."

But when the intellect was crushed beneath immensities, the soul rose up audaciously—flinging out into the seeming void its ineradicable belief in the Life whence it sprang— to find the void a plenum, Deity immanent throughout "empty" space.

Pantheism

Then pantheism unveiled its all-alluring beauties. The in-tercosmic God shone forth, dispelling all the clouds of doubt and fear and turning into gardens of delight the erstwhile desert sands. Had it come in its native garb, it would have won everyone. But to intellectual Europe the most generally recognized exponent of this theory was Spinoza. While his strong thought fascinated and compelled the intelligence, presented—as it often was by opponents—without the ethic based on it, it left the spirit starving and the heart cold. The idea got abroad that pantheism was a chill and stern phi-losophy, that its God was unconscious, inaccessible—the "Father" had disappeared. "God is a being absolutely in-finite; a substance consisting of infinite attributes, each of which expresses His eternal and infinite essence" (*Ethics*, Bk. I. Definition 6).

Of these attributes we know but two, extension and mind, or will. A summary of Spinoza's views is that God "is not a personal being, existing apart from the universe; but Him-self in His own reality. He is expressed in the universe, which is His living garment" (Firoude, *Short Studies*, p.

360). All things exist as He willed them to be; evil is not positive; there is "an infinite gradation in created things," "all in their way obedient."

Two things in Spinoza have repelled the emotions: his steady, logical, destructive analysis and calm acceptance of its results, and his theory of necessitarianism. The latter has been held fatal to morals, the former to devotion. Yet Spinoza was so far from being incapable of strenuous devotion that he was described by his enemies as "a God-intoxicated man," and his lofty, serene virtue and calm acquiescence in the Law of Life as he saw it were in themselves evidences of the fine fiber of his soul.

Western thought is swinging between pantheism and a more or less coherent theism; at one time thinkers are driven to accept the one infinite, self-existent Substance, impersonal, all-pervasive, and their emotions are chilled and paralyzed. At another time they expand in love and devotion to a consciously touched Father, and are checked by the logical contradictions in which they find themselves entangled. The compulsion of the intellect, the longings of the heart come out strongly in the poet who voiced so often the restless mentality of his age:

> The sun, the moon, the stars, the seas, the hills, and the
>   plains—
> Are not these, O Soul, the Vision of Him who reigns? . . .
>
> Earth, these solid stars, this weight of body and limb,
> Are they not sign and symbol of thy division from Him?
>
> Dark is the world to thee: thyself art the reason why;
> For is He not all but thou, that hast power to feel "I am
>   I"? . . .
>
> Speak to Him, thou, for He hears, and Spirit with Spirit
>   can meet—
> Closer is He than breathing, and nearer than hands and feet.
>
> Tennyson, Works, p. 277. Kegan Paul & Co.

In all Western forms of pantheism there is a common lack —the lack of the great ladder of beings stretching from the grain of dust to the loftiest spirit. All apparently end with humanity and see in it the highest expression of God, while humans, feeling their own littleness in the immensity of the God-pervaded universe, stretch out groping hands to find elder brothers, the outcome of evolution in past eternities, in other realms of space.

In none such exist, if an immeasurable past has brought as fruit no mighty beings far above our pigmy growth as we are above the mote in the sun's ray, must not all universes be but an ebb and flow of the ocean, in which we are but a bubble in the foam of a breaking wave? We see ourselves within measurable distance of our end, for why should our world bear a harvest for eternity when other like worlds have gone down into the past with no fruit remaining? The failure of the dead universes to produce continuing lives, exhibiting loftier powers, appears to prophesy for humanity an evolution equally limited, and to presage our approaching doom. Chilled by the dank vapors of annihilation, we fly back into the warmer regions of faith, and submit to any outrage on reason rather than stifle the ever-recurring conviction, "Not all of me shall die."

Divine Beings

Eastern pantheism comes to the rescue, satisfying head and heart alike. It is as impregnable intellectually as Spinoza, but solves the problems of life as can no philosopher who reduces intelligent beings to the narrow compass of humans and the lower kingdoms of nature.

Other disappearing worlds have left behind lives evolved by their aid; beings greater than humans, intelligences deeper, wider, loftier, crowd the realms of space, soaring to unimaginable grandeur. Angels of worlds, Gods of countless systems rise ever higher, with consciousness expanded to embrace vaster areas. They offer countless objects for worship, extending loving hands to help, the Fathers and Mothers of the systems that roll in space. They provide all that heart can long for, all that aspiration can soar to, all that reason can demand. The One Life pours out through each; in each is expressed some marvel of the otherwise unintelligible glory. They reveal part of That which eludes our grasping for totality. Some are so mighty and vast that they sustain a universe; some are individually so tender that a child, unafraid, might nestle on their breast.

In Eastern pantheism the One Life and the many Deities
are distinguished in thought, while the fundamental unity is
never out of sight. The many are but rays of the One,
manifested centers of consciousness, channels of the One,
each in its own measure. "He verily is all the Gods." "They
call him Indra, Mittra, Varuna, and Agni." "He who is
Brahma, who is Indra and Prajapati, is all these Gods."
(*Brihadaranyakopanishad*, Commentary on the Fourth
Brahmana, chap. i.)

The gods truly live as separate intelligences, but they no
more mar the divine unity than does the existence of human
beings as separate intelligences. To the philosophy of pantheism, polytheism adds the religious element needed for
spiritual evolution. Yet gods and humans, as well as all
other parts of the universe, live and move and have their being in the One. That is the One without a second, incognizable, infinite, the causeless Cause of Being. "It is beyond
the range and reach of thought—in the words of the *Man-
dukya*, 'unthinkable and unspeakable.'" (*The Secret Doctrine*, i. 42.) As salt in water, as butter in milk, the One Life
is in all, invisible to the eye but immanent in everything.

The symbol of That to our conditioned intelligence is the
supernal Trinity, Brahman in his threefold aspect, God in
manifestation, the highest point to which our thought can
soar. He is the One Self, and veils himself in innumerable
forms, amid which the "Seven Spirits" take the loftiest
place. Below them are many divine Beings, grouped in
threes and sevens according to their functions in any given
department of the cosmos. They also are referred to in many
other groupings familiar in world scriptures, yet reduci-
ble to the same fundamental complex units.* A three and a

---

*Thus in a seven the one is placed in the center and six are round it; this
doubled, the centers coinciding, gives twelve round the one; hence all
multiples of twelve. Again, the three taken as a center with the seven round
it yield ten, the decade (our system perfected at its close), and out of this
arise multiples of ten. Or, this central three being regarded as a unit, eight
represents the one and seven, and multiples of eight result. Further groupings appear when each of these threes and sixes or sevens is taken as double,
positive-negative, male-female, etc. But this number system in all its
ramifications is too big to deal with here.

seven form the rulers, it would seem, in many systems of our cosmos.

Below these are vast hierarchies of graduated intelligences, guiding the cosmic order, superintending its various departments, gods of the seven great elements, the permutations and combinations of which make up the material side of nature. The three *gunas* (qualities) and the seven *tattvas* (elements) compose the material side as the three Logoi, and the seven Spirits compose the life or energy side.

The Logos

When we think of the Logos as the Self of all, we think of him as One, as the Lord of the world and of humans. The highest Logos, we have heard, is One who has climbed the ladder of Being until he can hold his center of consciousness, himself unparalyzed and fully conscious, amid the mighty vibrations of the Great Life. Coming into manifestation, he limits himself to be the channel of that One Life to a universe.

The Logos has been human in an incalculable past, and has risen through every phase of superhuman being to the highest level of conditioned existence. Hence he can condition himself at any point of such existence. When for some gracious purpose he thus takes on the human condition and is born into one of his worlds, we call him an Avatara, a God-man. He lives again as a human on some globe, but the glory of Deity shines through him, and he is Emmanuel, God-with-us.

To such a one, or to any spiritual intelligence, those of all grades of head and heart can turn in worship, in love, in trust. From all such beings, we humans can ask for aid, counsel or guidance. The untrained brain cannot grasp the vast idea of an intracosmic God, all-pervasive, all-sustaining. The concept bewilders the intellect and chills the heart. Yet without love and trust and worship, the spiritual nature cannot awaken, cannot develop. It is not the object of worship but the attitude of the worshipper that rouses the emotions which stimulate spiritual growth. God is the life of every object, and it is he that is worshipped in each, not the outer form that is his veil. He is the all-attractive charm, the all-alluring power, and as the mind and heart of the worshipper expand and rise, form after form breaks away from him, each successive form showing more of his radiant loveliness, until he stands as manifest Lord of all, and the devotee made one with him becomes one with the Supreme.

Limited as we are at present, every conception of God we form is limited, inadequate, even grotesque in its imperfection. Well may we try in gentlest reverence to improve and purify conceptions lower and cruder than our own, recognizing that ours must be equally low and crude in the sight of those beyond us, however inspiring they may be to us at our less developed stage. Let us worship the highest we can dream in our purest moments, and strive to live the beauty we adore. Worship and life reveal God above us, because they awaken the powers of God within us. We become that which we worship and love. When the two become one in Nirvana the quest is over, the spark has become the Flame.

13

Discipleship

Much has been said and written on the qualifications for discipleship, as they are set down in Eastern scriptures. There they are laid down as the ideal according to which aspirants should try to shape their lives, and are intended to help candidates for discipleship by pointing to the direction in which they should turn their efforts. Hindus and Buddhists, to whom the qualifications were given, have always regarded them in this way, and aspirants have taken them as guides in self-culture, as pupils may strive to copy, to the best of their ability, the perfect statue set up in a class for study.

As these qualifications have become known in the Western world through theosophical literature, they have been used in a somewhat different spirit, as a basis for the criticism of others rather than as rules for self-education. It has been said that some people "used the bread of life as stones to cast at their enemies." The spirit that thus uses information is not uncommon among us. It may be open to question whether those who have spread through the world much information that once was kept secret may not occasionally have felt a twinge of doubt as to the wisdom of pouring forth teaching liable to so much misuse.

Our great teacher, H. P. Blavatsky, suffered much at the hands of those who use the qualifications for discipleship as missiles for attack, instead of as buoys to mark out the channel. It has been asked why a person who smoked, who lost her temper, who was lacking in self-control, should have been a disciple, while (this was not said but implied) many eminently respectable people, with all the family virtues, who never outrage conventionalities and are models of deportment, are not considered worthy of that title. It may not be useless to try to solve the puzzle.

Those who have read carefully the letters from those whom we call the Masters* must have sometimes been struck with surprise over the opinions the Masters expressed, as they envisage people and things so differently from the current appreciations in the world. They look at many things that to us seem important with utter indifference, and lay stress on matters that we overlook. Their surprising judgments teach readers a lesson of caution in the formation of opinions about others, and make one realize the wisdom of the teacher who said: "Judge not, that ye be not judged." A judgment which is not based on all the facts, which does not include knowledge of the causes from which actions spring, which rests on superficial appearances and not underlying motives is a judgment which is worthless. In the eyes of those who judge with knowledge, it condemns the judge rather than the victim. This is eminently true as regards the judgments passed on H. P. Blavatsky. It may be worthwhile to consider what is connoted by the words "disciple" and "initiate," and why she should have held the position of a disciple and an initiate, despite the criticisms showered upon her.

Discipleship Defined

Let us define our terms. "Disciple" is the name given in occult schools to those who, being on the probationary path, are recognized by some Master as attached to himself. The term asserts a fact, not a particular moral stage, and does not carry with it a necessary implication of the highest moral elevation. This comes out strongly in the traditional story of Jesus and his disciples: they quarrelled with each

---

*The Mahatma Letters, to A. P. Sinnett, compiled by A. T. Barker. Adyar, Madras, India: Theosophical Publishing House (1923) 1979.

other about precedence; they ran away when their Master was attacked; one of them denied him with oaths and later showed much duplicity.

The truth is that discipleship implies a past tie between Master and disciple. A Master may recognize that tie, growing out of past relationship, with one who has still much to achieve. The disciple may have many and serious faults of character and, though his or her face is turned to the Light, may by no means have exhausted all the heavy karma of the past. Disciples may be facing many a difficulty, fighting on many a battlefield with the legions of the past against them. The word "disciple" does not necessarily imply initiation or sainthood; it only asserts a position and a tie—that the person is on the probationary path and is recognized by a Master as his.

Among the people who occupy that position in the world today are many types. It is well for us to recall the law that we are what we desire and think, not what we do. What we desire and think shapes our future; what we do is the outcome of our past. Actions are the least important part of a person's life, from the occult standpoint—a hard doctrine to many, but true.

Certainly there is a karma connected with action. The past evil desire and thought, which are made manifest in an evil act in the present, have had their fruit in the shaping of tendencies and character. The act itself is expiated in the suffering and disrepute it entails; the remaining karma of the action grows out of its effect on others, and this reacts later in unfavorable circumstance.

Action, in the wide sense of the term, is composed of desire, thought and activity; the desire generates thought; the thought generates activity. The activity does not generate directly but only indirectly. Hence desires and thoughts are the most vital elements in forming a judgment passed on a person. What we desire, what we think, that we *are;* what we do, that we *were.*

It follows that those with heavy past karma may, if they become disciples, expedite the manifestation of that karma. Its fruit in the outer world may be actions that do not bring credit in the eyes of this world. From the occult standpoint, such people are to be helped to the utmost, so that they may be able to pass through the awful strain, which means triumph if they bear it successfully but failure if they succumb.

Moreover, in passing right judgments on someone's actions, we must not only know the actor's past in which the roots of the actions are struck, but we must know the immediate past, that which immediately preceded the action. Sometimes one does a wrong action only after a desperate struggle, in which he or she has put forth every ounce of strength in resistance. Only after complete exhaustion has the action been taken. From the outside we see the failure, not the struggle. But the struggler has profited by the efforts that preceded the failure and is the stronger, the nobler, the better for it. Such a person has developed the forces which will enable him or her to overcome the difficulty when it next presents itself, perhaps even without a struggle. In the eyes of those who see the whole and not only a fragment, that person who has been condemned as fallen has really risen, for he or she has won, as the fruit of the combat, the strength which assures victory.

Such disciples stand on the probationary path; they are candidates for initiation. They fall under conditions different from those that surround people in the outer world. They are recognized as pledged to the service of Light, and hence also recognized as opponents of the power of Darkness. Their joys will be keener, their sufferings sharper than normal. They have called down the fire from heaven; it is well for them if they do not shrink from its scorching. It is well for them, too, if, like the American Indian at the torture stake, they can face an unsympathetic world with a serene face, however sharply the fire may burn.

Qualifications for Initiation

What of the famous qualifications for initiation which disciples must now seek to make their own? These are not asked for in perfection, but there must be some of them present before the portal may swing open to admit one. In the judgment passed on disciples, which opens or bars the gateway, the whole person is taken into account. With some, other qualities are so greatly developed that only a small modicum of those specially demanded weighs down the scale in favor of the disciples. With others, generally more average, high development of the special requirements is demanded.

It is, so to speak, one's general stature that is looked at, and stature is made up in many ways. A candidate may be of great intelligence, of splendid courage, of rare self-sacrifice, of spotless purity, but lack somewhat in the special qualifications, though something of them must be present. If one had no sense of the difference between the real and unreal, was passionately addicted to the joys of the world, had no control over tongue or thought, no endurance, no faith, no liberality, no wish for freedom, he or she could not enter. The completion of the qualities may be left for the other side of the gates if their beginnings are seen. But the initiate must fill up the full tale, and the more that is lacking the more will need to be done.

It is not well to minimize the urgency of the demand, for these qualities must be reached sometime, and far better sooner than later. Every weakness that remains in the initiated disciple who has entered the path affords a point of vantage to the dark powers, who are ever seeking for crevices in the armor of the champions of the Light. No earnestness is too great in urging uninitiated disciples to acquire these qualities; no effort is too great on their part to achieve them. For there is something of pathos in the case of a hero-soul who has "taken the kingdom of heaven by storm," and then has to give a lifetime to building up lesser perfections which in the past he or she neglected to acquire.

> Though the mills of God grind slowly
>   Yet they grind exceeding small;
> Though He stands and waits with patience
>   With exactness grinds He all.

The lofty initiate who has left some minor parts of human perfection uncompleted must be born into the world to lead a life in which these also shall be perfected. If you should chance to meet such a one, you would be wise to learn from his or her best rather than to use the worst as excuse for your own shortcomings, thus trying to justify your own faults because you share them with an initiate.

H. P. Blavatsky

Preeminently is this true of the criticisms levelled against H. P. Blavatsky. "She smoked." But smoking is not a sin against the Holy Ghost. Using it to depreciate a great teacher is a far worse crime than smoking.

"She had a bad temper." So have a good many of her critics, who do not have a thousandth part of the excuse she well might have pleaded. Few could bear for a week the strain under which she lived year after year, with the dark forces storming around her, striving to break her down, because the breaking down would mean a check to the great spiritual movement which she led. In the position she was bidden to hold, the nervous strain and tension were so great, the cruel shafts of criticism and unkindness were rendered so stinging by the subtle craft of the Brothers of the Shadow, that she judged it better at times to relieve the body by an explosion. She sometimes let the jangled nerves express themselves in irritability rather than hold the body in strict subjection and let it break under the strain. At all hazards she had to live, with strained nerves and failing brain, till the hour struck for her release. It is wrong to criticize such a one, who suffered that we might profit.

"She lacked self-control." Outwardly sometimes, for the reasons given above, but never inwardly. Never was she shaken within, however stormy without. It may be said that such a statement could be used as an excuse for ill-temper in ordinary people. Let them stand where she stood, that is, become extraordinary people, and then they may fairly claim the same excuse.

H. P. Blavatsky was one of those who are so great, so priceless, that their qualities outweigh a thousandfold the temporary imperfections of their nature. Her dauntless courage, her heroic fortitude, her endurance in bearing physical and mental pain, her measureless devotion to the Master whom she served—these splendid qualities, united to great psychic capacities, and the strong body with nerves of steel that she laid on the altar of sacrifice, made all else as dust in the balance. Well might her Master take joy in such a warrior, even if she was not free from every imperfection. For those with little devotion and but small tendency to self-sacrifice, a strong manifestation of the special qualifications may well be demanded to counterbalance the deficiencies.

We worship the sun as a luminary and not for its spots. In the sunlight of H. P. Blavatsky's heroic figure, the spots are not what catch the eye of wisdom. But these spots do not raise to her level those who are nearly all spots, with but little gleams of light. It is foolish in these days of small virtues and small vices to criticize harshly the few great ones who may come into our world.

Often, with St. Catherine of Siena, have I felt that having intense love for someone even only a little higher than ourselves is one of the best methods for training ourselves into that lofty love of the Supreme Self which burns up all imperfections as by fire. Hero worship may have its dangers, but they are less perilous, less obstructive to the spiritual life, than the cold criticism of the self-righteous, directed constantly to depreciation of others. I hold with Giordano Bruno, the hero worshipper, that it is better to try greatly and fail than never to try at all.

14

Human Perfection

There is a stage in human evolution which immediately precedes the goal of all human effort. Those who pass through this stage have nothing more to accomplish as human beings. They have become perfect; their human career is over.

The great religions bestow different names on these Perfected Ones but whatever the name, the same idea is beneath it. Mithra, Osiris, Krishna, Buddha, Christ—all symbolize one made perfect. Such great Ones do not belong to a single religion, a single nation, a single human family. They are not stifled in the wrappings of a single creed; everywhere they are the most noble, the most perfect ideal. Every religion proclaims them; all creeds have their justification in them; such is the ideal towards which every belief strives. Each religion effectively fulfills its mission according to the clearness with which it illumines and the precision with which it teaches the road to reach the ideal.

The name of Christ, used for the Perfect One throughout Christendom, is the name of a *state,* more than the name of *man.* "Christ in you, the hope of glory" is the Christian teaching. We all, in the long course of evolution, reach the Christ state, for all accomplish in time the centuried pilgrimage. The one with whom the name is specially connected in Western lands is one of the Sons of God who have reached the final goal of humanity. The word "Christ" has always carried the connotation of a state; it is "the anointed." Each must reach the state: "Look within thee; thou art Buddha." "Till the Christ be formed in you."

As one who would become a musical artist should listen to the masterpieces of music, and become steeped in the melodies of master artists, so should we lift up our eyes and our hearts in contemplation to the mountains on which dwell the Perfect Ones of our race. What we are, they were; what they are, we shall be. All the sons of men can do what a Son of Man has accomplished. We see in them the pledge of our own triumph, the development of like divinity in us is but a question of evolution.

I have sometimes divided interior evolution into sub-moral, moral, and super-moral stages. In the sub-moral, the distinctions between right and wrong are not seen, and people follow their desires without question or scruple. In the moral, right and wrong are seen, become ever more defined and inclusive, and obedience to law is striven after. In the super-moral, external law is transcended because the divine nature rules its vehicles.

In the moral condition, law is recognized as a legitimate barrier, a salutary restraint. "Do this, avoid that." We struggle to obey, and there is a constant combat between the higher and the lower natures. In the super-moral state, the divine life finds its natural expression without external direction. We love, not because we ought to love, but because we are Love. We act, to quote the noble words of a Christian initiate, "not after the law of a carnal commandment, but by the power of an endless life." Morality is transcended when all our powers turn to the Good, as the magnetized needle turns to the north when Divinity in us seeks the best for all. There is no more combat, for the victory is won; the Christ has reached his perfect stature only when he has become the Christ triumphant, master of life and death.

The First Initiation

There are four degrees of development covered by the Christ-stage, between the thoroughly good person and the triumphant Master. Each of these degrees is entered by an initiation, and during these degrees of evolution consciousness is to expand, to grow, to reach the limits possible within the restrictions imposed by the human body.

The stage of the Christ-life, the Buddha-life, entered by the first of the great initiations, is one in which the initiate is "the little child," sometimes the "babe," sometimes the "little child, three years old." One must "regain the child-state he hath lost" and "become a little child" in order to "enter the kingdom." Passing through that portal, one is born into the Christ-life, and treading the "way of the Cross," passes onwards through the successive gateways on the Path. At the end, such a one is definitely liberated from the life of limitations, of bondage, and dies to time to live in eternity. The initiate becomes conscious of being life rather than form.

There is no doubt that in early Christianity this stage of evolution was definitely recognized as open to every individual Christian. The anxiety expressed by St. Paul that Christ might be born in his converts bears sufficient testimony to this fact, and there are passages that might be quoted. Even if this verse stood alone, it would suffice to show that in the Christian ideal the Christ-stage was regarded as an inner condition, the final period of evolution for every believer. It is well that Christians should recognize this, and not regard the life of the disciple, ending in perfection, as an exotic, planted in Western soil but native only in far Eastern lands. This ideal is part of all true and spiritual Christianity, and the birth of the Christ in each Christian soul is the object of Christian teaching. The very object of religion is to bring about this birth, and if this mystic teaching were to slip out of Christianity, that faith could no longer raise to Divinity those who practice it.

The first of the great initiations is the birth of the Christ, of the Buddha, in the human consciousness, the transcending of the I-consciousness and the falling away of limitations. The change experienced is the awakening of consciousness in the spiritual world, in the world where consciousness identifies itself with the life, and ceases to identify itself with the forms in which the life may at the moment be imprisoned. The characteristic of this awakening is a feeling of sudden expansion and of widening out beyond habitual limits. There is recognition of a Self, divine and puissant, which is Life, not form, joy, not sorrow. The feeling of a marvelous peace dawns, surpassing anything the world can dream of.

With the falling away of limitations comes an increased intensity of life, as though life flowed in from every side, rejoicing over the barriers being removed. So vivid is the feeling of reality that all life in a form seems as death, and earthly light as darkness. This is an expansion so marvelous that consciousness feels as though it had never known itself before, for what was regarded as consciousness is as unconsciousness in the presence of this upwelling life.

Self-consciousness commenced to germinate in child-humanity, and has always developed, grown, expanded within the limitations of form. It has thought itself separate, feeling as "I," speaking of "me" and "mine." This self-consciousness suddenly feels all selves as Self, all forms as common property. Those who experience this see that limitations were necessary for building a center of selfhood in which self-identity might persist. At the same time they feel that the form is only an instrument for their use, while the living consciousness is one with all that lives.

The initiate knows the full meaning of the phrase "the unity of humanity," and feels what it is to live in all that lives and moves. This consciousness is accompanied with an immense joy, that joy of life which even in its faint reflections upon earth is one of the keenest ecstasies known to humanity. The unity is not only seen by the intellect, but it is felt as satisfying the yearning for union known by all who have loved. It is a unity felt from within, not seen from without. It is not a conception, but a life. The story of the birth of the Christ in us has been told since ancient times. And yet words shaped for the world of forms fail to image the world of Life.

The child must grow into the perfect adult. There is much to do, much weariness to face, many sufferings to endure, many combats to wage, many obstacles to overcome before the Christ born in the feebleness of infancy may reach the stature of the Perfect One. There is the life of labor among one's fellows; there is the facing of ridicule and suspicion; there is the delivery of a despised message; there is the agony of desertion, the passion of the Cross and the darkness of the tomb. All these lie before the disciple on the path he or she has entered.

Practicing Unity

By continual practice, disciples must learn to assimilate the consciousness of others. They must center their own consciousness in Life, not in form, so that they may pass beyond the "heresy of separateness," which makes them regard others as different from themselves. They have to expand their consciousness by daily practice, until its normal state is that which they temporarily experienced at the first initiation.

To this end they will endeavor in everyday life to identify their consciousness with the consciousness of those with whom they come into contact day by day. They will strive to feel as others feel, to think as they think, to rejoice as they rejoice, to suffer as they suffer. Gradually disciples must develop a perfect sympathy, a sympathy which can vibrate in harmony with every string of the human lyre. Gradually they must learn to answer, as if it were their own, to every sensation of another, however high or low. Gradually by constant practice they must identify with others in all the varied circumstances of their different lives. They must learn the lesson of joy and the lesson of tears, and this is only possible when one has transcended the separated self and no longer asks for anything, but understands that henceforth life must be lived for life alone.

The first sharp struggle for disciples is to put aside all that up to this point has been for them life, consciousness, reality, and to walk forth alone, naked, no longer identifying themselves with any form. They have to learn the law of life, by which alone the inner Divinity can manifest, the law which is the antithesis of the past. The law of form is taking; the law of life is giving. Life grows by pouring itself out through form, fed by the inexhaustible source of life at the heart of the universe. The more the life pours itself out, the greater the inflow from within. It seems at first to young Christs as though all their life were leaving them, as though their hands were left empty after pouring out their gifts to a

thankless world. Only when the lower nature has been definitely sacrificed is the eternal life experienced, and that
which seemed the death of being is found to be a birth into a
fuller life.

The Second Initiation

Thus consciousness develops, until the first stage of the
Path is trodden, and disciples see before them the second
portal of initiation, symbolized in the Christian scriptures as
the Baptism of the Christ. At this, as they descend into the
waters of the world's sorrows, the river in which every savior must be baptized, a new flood of divine Life is poured
out upon them. Their consciousness realizes itself as the Son,
in whom the life of the Father finds fit expression. They feel
the life of the monad, the Father in heaven, flowing into
their consciousness, and realize that they are one, not only
with humanity, but also with the heavenly Father. They
realize that they live on earth only to be the expression of the
Father's will, his manifested organism. Henceforth is their
ministry to others the most patent fact in life. They are the
Son, to whom people should listen, because the hidden Life
flows from them. They have become a channel through
which that hidden Life can reach the outer world. They are
priests of the Mystery God, who have entered within the veil
and come forth with glory shining from their faces, the
reflection of the Light in the sanctuary.

It is there that the work of love begins, symbolized in the
outer ministry by willingness to heal and to relieve. Souls
seeking Light and Life press around the disciples, attracted
by their inner force and by the Divine Life manifested in the
accredited Son of the Father. Hungry souls come to them
and are given bread; souls suffering from the disease of sin
come, and are healed by the living word; souls blinded by
ignorance come and are illuminated by wisdom. It is one of
the signs of a Christ in his or her ministry that the abandoned and the poor, the desperate and the degraded, come
without a sense of separation. They feel a welcoming sympathy and are not repelled; for kindness radiates from such
persons, and the love that understands flows out around
them. Truly, those who come are ignorant and do not know

that these are evolving Christs. But they feel a power that raises, a life that vitalizes, and in their atmosphere they breathe in new strength, new hope.

The Third and Fourth Initiations

Now before disciples is the third portal, which admits them to another stage of progress, and they have a brief moment of peace, of glory, of illumination, symbolized in Christian writings by the Transfiguration. It is a pause, a brief cessation of active service, a journey to the mountain where the peace of heaven broods. There—as they stand side by side with some who have recognized the evolving Divinity—that Divinity shines forth for a moment in its transcendent beauty.

During this lull in the combat, disciples see their future. A series of pictures unrolls before their eyes. They behold the sufferings which lie before them, the solitude of Gethsemane, the agony of Calvary. Then their faces are set steadfastly towards Jerusalem, towards the darkness they are to enter for the love of humankind.

They understand that before they can reach the perfect realization of unity, they must experience the quintessence of solitude. Earlier, while conscious of the growing life, it seemed to come to them from without. Now they are to realize that its center is within. In the solitude of the heart they must experience the true unity of the Father and the Son, an interior and not an outer unity. For this, all external contact with others, and even with God, must be cut off so that within their own Spirit they may find the One.

As the dark hour approaches, disciples are more and more appalled by the failure of the human sympathies on which they had relied during the past years of life and service. When, in the critical moment of need, they look around for comfort and see their friends wrapped in indifferent slumber, it seems that all human ties are broken, that all human love is a mockery, all human faith a betrayal. Disciples are flung back upon themselves to learn that only the tie with the Father in heaven remains, that all embodied aid is useless.

It has been said that in this hour of solitude the soul is

filled with bitterness, and that rarely a soul passes over this gulf of voidness without a cry of anguish. It is then that the agonized reproach bursts forth: "Couldst thou not watch with me one hour?" But no human hand may clasp another in that Gethsemane of desolation.

When this darkness of human desertion has passed, then, despite the human nature shrinking from the cup, comes deeper darkness. In this hour a gulf seems to open between the Father and the Son, between the embodied life and the Infinite Life. The Father, who was yet realized in Gethsemane when all human friends were slumbering, is veiled in the passion of the Cross. It is the bitterest of all the ordeals of the initiate. Even consciousness of the life of Sonship is lost, and the hour of the hoped-for triumph becomes that of the deepest ignominy. Initiates see their enemies exultant around them, themselves abandoned by friends and lovers. They feel the divine support crumble away beneath their feet. They drink to the last drop the cup of solitude, of isolation. No contact with humans or with God bridges the void in which hang their helpless souls. Then from the heart that feels itself deserted even by the Father, rings out the cry: "My God! My God! Why has *Thou* forsaken me?"

Why this last proof, this last ordeal, this most cruel of all illusions? It *is* illusion, for the dying Christ is nearest of all to the divine heart.

This comes because the Sons must know themselves to be one with the Father they seek, must find God not only within but as their innermost self. Only when initiates know that the Eternal is themselves and they are Eternal are they beyond the possibility of the sense of separation. Then, and then only, can they perfectly help the human race and become a conscious part of the uplifting energy.

The Fifth Initiation

The Christ triumphant, the Christ of the Resurrection and Ascension, has felt the bitterness of death, has known all human suffering. He has risen above it by the power of his own divinity. What can now trouble his peace or check his hand outstretched to help? During his evolution he learned to receive into himself the currents of human troubles and to send them forth again as currents of peace and joy. Within the circle of his activity, this was his work, to transmute forces of discord into forces of harmony. Now he must do it for the world, for the humanity out of which he has flowered.

The Christs and their disciples, in the measure of their evolution, thus protect and help the world. The struggles would be far bitterer, the combats of humanity far more desperate, were it not for the presence of those whose hands bear up "the heavy karma of the world."

Even those who are at the earliest stage of the Path become lifting forces in evolution, as in truth are all who unselfishly work for others, though those on the Path more deliberately and continuously. But the Christ triumphant does completely what others do at varying stages of imperfection; therefore he is called a "Savior," and this characteristic in him is perfect. He saves, not by substituting himself for us, but by sharing his life with us. He is wise, and we are all the wiser for his wisdom, for his life flows into our veins and pulses in our hearts. He is not tied to a form, nor separate from any. He is the Ideal Man, the Perfect Man. Each human being is a cell in his body, and each cell is nourished by his life.

Surely it would not have been worthwhile to suffer the Cross and to tread the Path that leads to it simply for Christ to win his own liberation a little earlier, to be at rest a little sooner. The cost would have been too heavy for such a gain, the strife too bitter for such a prize. In his triumph humanity is exalted, and the path trodden by all feet is rendered a little shorter. The evolution of the whole race is accelerated; the pilgrimage of each is made less long. This was the thought that inspired him in the violence of the combat, that sustained his strength, that softened the pangs of loss. There is not one being—however feeble, however degraded, however ignorant, however sinful—who is not a little nearer to the Light when a Son of the Highest has finished the course. How the speed of evolution will be quickened as more and more of these Sons rise triumphant, and enter into conscious Life Eternal! How swiftly will the wheel turn, lifting us into Divinity, as more and more of us become consciously divine!

Herein lies the stimulus for each of us who, in our noblest moments, has felt the attraction of life poured out for love of humanity. Let us think of the sufferings of the world that does not know why it suffers; of the misery, the despair of those who do not know why they live and why they die; who, day after day, year after year, see sufferings fall upon themselves and others and do not understand the reason; who fight with desperate courage or furiously revolt against conditions they cannot comprehend or justify. Let us think of the agony born of blindness, of the darkness in which such people grope, without hope, without aspiration, without knowledge of the true life, and of the beauty beyond the veil. Let us think of the millions of our brothers and sisters in the darkness, and then of the uplifting energies born of our sufferings, our struggles and our sacrifices. We can raise others a step towards the Light, alleviate their pains, diminish their ignorance, abridge their journey towards the knowledge which is Light and Life. Which of us who knows even a little would not give himself or herself for these who know nothing?

We know by the immutable law, by unswerving truth, by the endless Life of God, that all Divinity is within us. Though it is now but little evolved, infinite capacity is there, available for uplifting the world. Surely, then, there is not one able to feel the pulsing of the Divine Life who is not attracted by the hope to help and bless.

If this Life is felt, however feebly, for however brief a time, it is because in the heart is the first thrill of that which will unfold as the Christ-life, because the time approaches for the birth of the Christ-babe, because in such a one humanity is seeking to flower.

15

The Future that Awaits Us

Can you picture human evolution, leading you onwards to the future that lies before the human race? I will endeavor to guide you step by step—though the steps will be somewhat long ones—up the staircase which, through the ages, the race will climb. In order to do this intelligently, I must carry your thoughts backwards briefly. It is necessary to glance at our long past as a preliminary reminder, even for those who already know the facts, in order that we may have the whole great scheme before us from the beginning to the end of the manvantara.

Past Evolution

Think for a moment, as far as thought is possible, of that high region of the beginning of a universe. From the great Logos from whom the universe proceeded, there issues a Breath which comes forth and returns but once in a manvantara. This is the mighty Life-Breath in which all systems, all worlds, all individuals live, breathe, and exist. Let there be in your mind for a moment a picture of that vast cycle of evolution—evolution as yet unaccomplished, evolution existing in the thought of the Logos but not in the facts of manifestation.

Then, running swiftly onwards from that beginning, place before your minds another picture, that of the making of the planes of a universe, region after region. The energy of the Logos, flashing forth, pours itself out as Atma, the one Self, into a universe yet to be. It makes plane after plane in sevenfold order. It is itself the energy, the first spirit; the

145

first matter is its own outer aspect, the ring within which it limits itself for the purpose of manifestation. This energy passes outwards, enfolded in that first matter as in a garment. Its outer aspect again forms a new phase of matter, that of the second plane, so that the energy of the second plane is the first energy *plus* first-plane matter. Around this the fresh differentiation of the matter of the second plane is wrapped. The energy of the third plane is the first energy *plus* first and second-plane matter, and the outer limit becomes third-plane matter. Thus region after region is made, until the seven (the root-number of this universe) are complete. All are differentiations of the One—all Atma, but Atma modifying itself in manifestation.

Then, touching the limiting surface of the sphere—the self-ordained ring pass-not—the great Life-wave rushes back upon itself, drawing in from circumference to center. Having touched the outermost limit, the lowest world of matter, it begins to unfold what it had infolded.

Having thus brought into objective existence the spirit-matter of each plane, the Life-wave begins to use this as material. It builds that spirit-matter into various organisms and forms of living things that are to be vehicles of consciousness in this universe. They are ultimately to be fit to form the living temples of the undifferentiated Atma as it streams forth as the energy of the Logos. The unfolding energy climbs from mineral to vegetable, from vegetable to animal, and so upwards to precursors of humanity. Imagine this vast aeonian succession, and see how in these bodies, which the undifferentiated Atma is brooding over, unfold one by one the successive types of spirit-matter. These had been infolded during the descent. Imagine how, going upwards to the animal and yet further to early human beings —more animal than human—gradually these subtler, less dense types of spirit-matter unfold within the coarser matter of the physical body. These subtle energies belong to the different planes formed by the infolding of the Life.

The Birth of Humanity

At last the moment comes when full human beings begin to be. This upward-climbing, unfolding energy is now able to stretch upwards to the ever-living Fire that flashes downwards from above, and the life below reaches up to the life above, till they meet and humanity is born.

Let me help you with a simile drawn from everyday experience. You know how the electric arc is formed, the blazing light of the electric lamp. Two carbon poles—one positive, the other negative—come nearer and nearer to each other in the darkness. At last they are so near to each other that the resistance of the air is overcome, and the current springs from pole to pole. The electric arc is formed, and light blazes forth.

That electric arc may serve as a symbol of the sudden formation of the individual, the real human being. An individual is born when what we may call the negative current of Atma reaching upwards and the positive current of Atma reaching downwards rush together and meet. The immortal Self comes into existence, to live through the measureless ages of eternity.

All this is just enough to remind you of what lies behind us in the past, of facts which must be clear in your mind if you are to see the future that awaits us, the future which I will try to sketch.

This great Life-Breath, then, is sweeping on, and humanity is beginning to be. That wave is the wave of evolution, the Law by which all must live, the progress by which all is carried onwards. This includes ourselves as well as the planet on which we live, the universe and all the worlds in it. All that goes with this current is carried onward and upward; all that sets itself against it is cast downward as wreckage, to be worked up again in some far-off future in which all missed possibilities shall be realized.

We may think of humanity now as the individual beginning to climb upward and coming to the place at which we stand today. In order to make a difficult subject a little clearer, let me ask you to image the three great kinds of activities in which we progress. I could fancy them as a mighty three-sided pyramid, with the upward-pointing apex piercing heaven. Each side of the pyramid typifies one of the three great activities of the universe: one side is power, another wisdom, another love. Within these all minor activities group themselves, all possibilities are included.

On the sides of the pyramid you may see figured many lines that seem parallel but are really convergent. These are the varied lines of progress—mental, moral, spiritual— along which humanity is to evolve. If you think of this pyramid as made of blocks, each block a great stage of progress symbolizing one of the regions of the universe, then at the base we should have the physical world. Working there, all the human powers and energies are manifested as physical consciousness in the physical body. The three sides of human nature—power, wisdom, and love—are gradually evolving.

Next above, is the second great block symbolizing the astral plane, another great region to be occupied by human consciousness. Above that is the plane of Manas—the devachanic plane, the region of the mind itself. Above that lies a region yet nobler and loftier, that of Buddhi or spiritual intuition, the plane of Samadhi, sometimes called Sushupti. Above that is the plane of Atma, Nirvana, the crown, enfolding all, within all.

To think of this picture may help as we pass from step to step, from block to block, for we have to trace humankind rising from stage to stage, in order to understand what human evolution consists of.

Our evolution consists in expanding consciousness, consciousness beginning at the very base of our pyramid as a mere thread of living light. It expands as it mounts from region to region, widening out and taking in more and more. At last the thread becomes a cone of fire, and it rises to the very apex and joins the ocean of living Fire in which all Light and all Life reside.

Expansion of consciousness is the hallmark of human evolution. As consciousness expands, taking more and more within its limits, humankind thus rising will increase in power, wisdom and love. These three cannot really be disjoined except for clearness of explanation, for love is but the outward expression of wisdom, and power its effectual agent. Still, considering each separately may help to systematize our thinking, and that is advantageous in a subject so complex and so difficult.

The Physical Plane

Taking the human race as a whole, we may say that its self-conscious life is in the body on the physical plane. Humanity as before defined may indeed be said to have come down from higher regions into physical encasement. But those regions are not yet subdued by consciousness for most people, and humankind at large cannot be said to live at present in self-conscious activity in them. Humans inhabit them, but their consciousness in them is the consciousness of a babe, not yet awake.

Still, so that mistake may not arise, let me say that there are even now some who have risen above the physical plane and are able to work on other planes, and they are in ever-increasing numbers. In all that I may say of the future, I shall speak of nothing that is not known to at least one or two among us who have gained a partial realization of the future of the race, who know at least something of these different planes, which in the future all shall know perfectly and possess fully.

In glancing over the physical region, how do its activities group themselves on the three sides of our pyramid? On the side of love we have service to those above us and help and compassion to those around and below us. On the side of wisdom we have that which is not yet wisdom but only knowledge, yet knowledge that will become wisdom when it is transmuted. Science, philosophy and art are the great lines along which thought is ascending on the side of wisdom. On the side of power we have government, rule, the organization of society and that creative power that even now resides in all people, even though as yet they do not know it.

The Limits of Physical Life

It may strike you as strange, almost startling, that on each of these sides we seem to be reaching the limits of the physical, continually coming to walls we are unable to leap over. We have a successful past behind us, no doubt, yet it seems as though progress in the physical is over, and something else must be found if success is to continue. If we look at the region of love—which has religion and the service of those above us for one of its lines of growth—we see that the great religions of the world have been pushed back by the advancing tide of skeptical intelligence, so that they are now in a position of extreme difficulty. Even those who love them most feel doubt in the back of their minds as to whether they are on the right road. It is recognized that in the great domain of religion, faith has too much taken the place of knowledge, hope too much the place of certainty and authority too much the place of vision. The result is that—go to what country you may, take what religion you please— you find the great masses of the people sunk in superstition, a prey to terrors of every kind. The unknown future in front of them is terror-filled because unknown.

Where there is not superstition among the masses, there is atheism, eating away ideals. And in addition to this religious degradation of the crowd, there is a class of more highly educated people, skeptical at heart and in life if not always in word, but often skeptical in word as well. They challenge religion because they know that its mere exoteric presentation cannot be intelligently held as true in fact. They challenge all and find no hope of a truth that may be realized beneath the challenge, though they feel the ground giving way beneath their feet.

If we turn to the other line on the side of love—helpful activity and compassion to those around and below us—we see a few brave hearts overwhelmed, despairing before the mass of human misery which they are incompetent to meet or heal. They see poverty, heart-breaking as to the body, and ignorance, more heart-breaking as to the mind, so that those who love humanity scarcely know from what direction effective aid may come.

On the side of wisdom, also, dead walls meet our gaze on each ascending line. Science, which has accomplished so

many triumphs, is apparently reaching the limit of the exquisite delicacy and accuracy of its physical apparatus. Yet
there come pouring into the laboratories energies too subtle
for its measures to gauge, substances too rare for its balances
to weigh. Science on every side is groping after new methods. In medicine it finds itself blind, doctors unable to
diagnose disease for lack of clearness of vision, unable to
trace definitely the action of drugs, merely experimenting,
and ever hoping that out of experiments some certain
knowledge may emerge. In physical science materialism is
breaking down, with its theories of the universe proved to
be inadequate, while idealism is not ready to take its place
to speak clearly and to explain intelligibly.

In the greatest of idealistic systems, the Vedanta of India,
as it is now taught, we find intellect devoted to useless hair-
splitting instead of profound thinking, a subtle deterioration
of character, and modes and habits of thought which undermine morals. Its students are becoming careless of conduct
in life and of the difference between right and wrong, self-
hypnotized by an unintelligent repetition of the profound
truth, "Thou art That." In East and West alike are blindness and gropings, a vague craving that knows only that it
has lost its ideals and that where there are no ideals truth
cannot be.

And power. What shall we say of the human activities
that play on the side of power? Society at war within itself,
class against class, sex against sex; kings with no authority to
control, who no longer reign, who have no responsibility, to
whom has been left the social power to do evil while the
governing power to do good has been wrested from them.
The power torn from them has been placed in the hands of a
many-millioned ignorance, in some vague hope that this
will pull in so many directions that no very harmful movement will occur. As a result moral and physical deterioration are visible everywhere, poverty and misery nearly in-
vincible, with no wisdom that is able to guide, no power
that ventures to control. People look dimly backward and
fearfully forward, wondering when a social cataclysm will

occur. Some dream sadly of the days when there were kings who were initiates and who gathered the nations under the safe shelter of their thrones, where knowledge and power grew into mighty life and realized a true society. And what of the power of creation? But, as I said, that is now unknown, and it is useless to speak of it.

Well, let us glance forwards, and see how humanity shall advance to greater peace, security and happiness on this physical plane. All the changes that will come into the physical plane in the future will come from the working downwards of the higher powers that will then be generally evolved in humankind.

The Astral World

We can now picture to ourselves the nearest step, that into the second region—human mounting to the second great stage of our pyramid. People will become self-conscious on the astral plane, conquering the astral realm, and will thus find a new world. Here they will acquire new powers, adopt new methods; new vistas will open, new potentialities blossom forth on every side. It is the race that is rising, not merely stray individuals that are outstripping their fellows.

Let us try to realize this next stage in human progress, when the majority will have expanded from self-consciousness in the physical to self-consciousness in the astral world. Let us see how humanity will evolve and grow along the lines that we have considered in the physical world.

What is this astral world, and what do we mean by the expanding of consciousness to embrace this second region in the universe? First, there is expansion of sense-power. The astral senses, while still distinguishable from each other—for we are not beyond walls of separation in the astral world —are not so limited as the physical. Astral vision sees behind, before and around; it sees every side of an object and pierces through it. The senses acquire fresh subtlety, acuteness and refinement, and from every direction wider knowledge pours in through these wider windows of the soul. The keener, stronger senses pierce through and overcome the obstacles that hindered humanity when consciousness could work only through the physical body.

The Love Side of the Pyramid

Taking up the activities on the side of love to the service of those above us, we find that when people pass into the astral world they will see and investigate phenomena that they only dreamed of or took on faith when restricted to the physical world. They will first come into touch with great truths, great realities, mighty Intelligences in this astral world. The awakening consciousness may only touch the fringe and not yet understand the nature of these, but this touch will make them real and no longer only matters of faith.

When this unknown world opens up before the awakened vision of most, as it is now open only to the few, people will find that they are not only able to see with far-reaching vision, not only able to use astral senses in the physical body, but can leave the physical body whenever it is an inconvenience or a hindrance. They can use the astral body to travel through the astral world.

Then it will be possible to communicate with the great Intelligences who may be reached when the limits of the physical are overstepped. Religion will take on new life, for the very basis of skepticism will be struck away when people can see and investigate phenomena now wrongly deemed supernatural, and when they again come into direct touch with beings whose very existence is now denied.

So also must superstition disappear when people can at will range the world beyond the grave. That which is no longer the unknown will cease to be a land of terrors, and fears will no more be played upon by those who seek to subjugate the ignorant through dread of the unseen world. All will know that world and understand its phenomena, marvelous now, but familiar and part of daily life then. What we call death will be practically shorn of its sorrows, for people will be able to live in the astral world and mingle with those who have shaken off for a time the limitations of the physical body. The astral world will have come within the compass of the ordinary life, and the division caused by death will be swept away.

People will be able to contact the great Ones and the teaching that then will be thrown open to the world. Space does not have power to divide, in view of the swiftness of passage in that subtler region. Thus, opportunities of knowledge that today come only to the very few will be in reach of all, knowledge that will change the whole aspect of life and open up still diviner possibilities.

There, too, people will meet the great teachers of the past, and will know that they are not dreams but living beings. They will see all that has been taught of these as noble is true, while all that ignorance has done to obscure them will face away in that brighter light, in the clearer vision of that purer day.

When we turn from the line of religion to that of help to those around us and compassion to those below, what will not humanity be able to accomplish when a majority can do what only a minute minority can do now! People will be able to grasp the astral forces and use them constantly both in the physical and the astral worlds.

In the physical world a people will be able to aid and protect others, by consciously sending forces from the astral to effect this purpose. They will be able to think a useful thought and clothe it in elemental essence, thus creating an artificial elemental which can be directed to help the weaker, to safeguard the unprotected, to ward off danger. Such forces form a continual shield for anyone to whom they are sent.

All this will be within the easy reach of those who are the vanguard of human evolution. The most backward will be aided by those who have advanced further, all these powers coming within the reach of the majority. Help to all who need it in the astral world will also be given, help to all the souls of the backward ones who, on casting off the physical body, for the first time enter a world that is new to them. For people will not be equal then any more than they are

equal now. The great majority will be working self-consciously on the astral plane, but there will still be vast
numbers whose consciousness will not have risen to it. The
majority will be available from which to draw helpers to
guide, comfort and direct the more ignorant souls who have
cast off the garment of the physical body. The majority will
do the work that only the few do now.

There are great opportunities upon the astral plane today, for even now comfort may be brought to the souls that
go there helpless, hurried into that region full of fear. Their
terrors may be soothed, their minds enlightened. In the future this blessed work will lie open to all who reach these
higher possibilities along the line of compassion.

Another blessing that will come to the world, working
down from the astral to the physical plane, will be along the
line of the education of the children. How will education be
changed when the astral senses are awakened? When the
minds of children lie open before their parents and teachers?
When their characters are plainly limned in color and form,
as they are to astral vision? When all their evil tendencies
are recognized in the germ in childhood and are starved,
while all the good ones are helped and strengthened, encouraged to blossom? The education of children in the future—which, after all, is not so far away—will make their
progress a thousandfold swifter than it is today. What might
not be done for children if they were trained by those with
astral vision—if all seeds of vice were starved, if all seeds of
good were encouraged? Instead of seeing youngsters grow
up as mere copies of the elder people around them, we
should see them growing up as a truly new generation, unfolding the possibilities that even now are within. The
ignorance that encourages the evil and discourages the good
is deplorable. It is a blindness that is as a bandage on the
eyes of our people, so that they are unable to see and
therefore to guide the young.

The Wisdom Side

When we turn from the side of love to that of wisdom, we
find that with the expansion of consciousness on the astral

plane a complete change must occur. The methods of science will be altered, the old methods that already are beginning to be outworn will be cast aside in favor of keener and subtler tools. Scientists will use these better instruments of the astral senses in order to study and understand the phenomena of the physical world, as well as those of the astral world. I can indicate only a few of the new methods that will then come into common use, but a brief indication will show you how wide their scope is.

Take medical science. Imagine the difference in certainty and precision when the doctor diagnoses by vision and traces the action of drugs by astral sight. Neither physicians nor surgeons will be shut out by the surface of things as they are today, but every doctor will see exactly what is at fault and will apply remedies accordingly.

Or take the methods of chemistry. Chemists will no longer theorize, but they will see. Atoms will no longer be possibilities and abstractions but things that can be easily examined and traced.* All combinations will be studied with astral vision, stage after stage watched and followed. Chemists will tests, dissociate, combine, rearrange, all with the certainty that comes from vision, and they will manipulate materials by the new forces at their command.

In psychology how changed will be the methods when the mind lies before psychologists as an open book. Instead of speculating on mind in animals, drawing inferences from their actions, guessing at their motives, researchers will see the way in which the animal is thinking, the strange world that dawns on the animal intelligence—a world so different from our own because the standpoint from which it is seen is so different. Then we will indeed be able to deal effectively with the animal mind, training the dawning intelligence, guiding its advance with clear and competent knowledge.

Thought will be studied as it is sent from mind to mind, and psychology will no longer be a jumble of words, a grouping of unenlightened ideas. The whole will fall into order gradually and be understood and mastered, for psy-

---

*See Occult Chemistry: Annie Besant and C. W. Leadbeater.

chologists will then know in what the human mind consists, and will begin to understand how it works and the possibilities of its unfolding powers.

Think too of philosophy. There will no longer be any possibility of discussion as to its basis in view of the wider knowledge, of powers before uncredited, of matter with potentialities unimagined, matter found to be so much subtler than had been thought possible, but still ever acting as a garment for the life. Then what is now lacking in idealism will be supplied—the understanding of the relationship between force and matter as the two aspects of the One, between life and the garment in which life is clothed. We will comprehend further how matter is subject to the life, how it assumes the form that thought commands, how the creative power is able to function, though this will be grasped far more fully in the regions beyond the astral.

Consider also the writing of history. How different that will be in a world where all the astral records lie open to be read. Then history can no longer be written from one side or the other, to support a theory or to bolster some view of the writer. Those who are historians will throw themselves back into the past and live and move among the scenes which they depict! When history is told, it will be told from the astral records, the living scenes, and they who tell it will live as if in the period, and trace events step by step with the men and women of the time. And all this will have the certainty of observation—reverified at will by different students. Neither guess nor inference will be necessary, only patient looking and faithful recording. Just as we live and move among our fellows today the historian will live and move in the world we call the past, a world living and present to those who know how to tread their way in it.

Again, how different will art be in those days that are coming—different even from the merely mechanical standpoint. So many more colors will then delight the eye, brilliant and vivid of hue, translucent, exquisite and soft. There are such varieties of changing forms in the astral world, so much more to delineate, to reproduce. Even down in the physical world the canvas of the painter will glow with the beauties of the astral. And when musicians write great symphonies or marvelous sonatas, they will not only breathe forth sounds to charm the ears, but colors will flash out as the notes fall sweetly. Every symphony will be a dazzling series of colors as well as of sounds, with a beauty that is now undreamed of, with a perfection and a delicacy as yet unknown.

The Side of Power

From the side of wisdom, let us pass to the side of power. In the future the ancient basis of society will be replaced with better materials for its builders' hands. Each of the different functions of a perfectly ordered state will be discharged by those who are fitted for them by natural evolution. Everyone's aura* will be visible to those who guide the state, and the duty each is called on to discharge will be according to the knowledge and power and benevolence visible to astral sight.

We all have the delineation of our character and powers around us in our auras, marking the functions we are best suited to perform, so that each will then be sent to his or her rightful place. A feeling that justice is done will make people harmonious, knowing that they are doing that for which they are fitted. They will have confidence in that power which sees and gives them ranks and marks out the region of their activity.

Most people will be able to see for themselves, and will endorse the justice of the ruling authority. Those who cannot see will be kept in check by the overwhelming public opinion. Then knowledge will rule ignorance, and power will shield and guide impotence. People will laugh at the insane idea that the multiplication of ignorance is wisdom.

In those days, as youths are growing into adulthood their paths in life will be selected, according to the color, fineness and size of their auras, which will show—as they show now

---

*The aura is an ovoid of colored lights that surrounds the physical body, visible to clairvoyants. A person's character is reflected in the aura, See C. W. Leadbeater, *Man Visible and Invisible*, and Dora Kunz, *The Personal Aura.*—ED.

to those whose eyes are opened—the range their faculties can cover and the powers they have within them for development. Then work will be joy, as all work is joy when it is fitted to the powers of the worker. The labor, the pain of work come when it frustrates powers which we possess, when the work is not fitted to the capacity. When people are doing that for which their faculties are best suited, there will be harmony and content in society instead of discontent and threats of revolution.

In those days how different also will be the law, especially as to criminal jurisprudence. As soon as astral sight becomes a power common to even a strong minority, there must be an entire change in dealing with evil and evil-doers. If people possessed astral sight now, it would not be possible for them to do many of the things that are done by nations and by society at the present time. It would not be possible for nation to fling itself against nation in war, for then many would perceive the misery and disturbance brought into the astral world by the soul hurled there in terror and wrath. And there could be no such thing as capital punishment among people who could trace the afterlife, and who would know that every murderer set free by execution can injure society more effectually than when he or she is bound within the body.

Then, too, humans will take up their duty towards the animal kingdom as well as towards their own brothers and sisters. Those with astral vision could not act towards animals as blindly as people do now. In a civilized world there will be no slaughter-houses, no butcher shops, with their surroundings of loathsome elemental creatures and astral forms of animals driven from their physical bodies in fear and horror. As people slay these helpless creatures, they send back into the world they left vibrations of distrust and hatred of humans, affecting the animals living upon the earth and bringing about the "instinctive" repulsion which so largely marks the attitude of the animal world towards humans. In those days the crime called "sport" will no longer disgrace humankind, staining with innocent blood the hands that should be pure. Human beings will cease to be the chief agents who bring misery into the world. When once they see what they are doing, these evils will be swept away forever.

Thus as humanity rises in self-consciousness to the astral world, wonderful changes will come about that will alter the whole face of society. They will make the earth far fairer. Love, wisdom and power will have been developed along the lines we have considered, and along many others as well.

The Region of the Mind

Another stage arises now before our eyes—the devachanic world, the region of the mind itself. The time will come when humankind shall rise into that loftier consciousness and be able to function in the devachanic body and use the devachanic senses.

How shall I tell of the possibilities of that wondrous world, of all its marvels, its flashing colors and melodious sounds, its intense life and radiant light? How shall any idea of it be given except in its own language? For there speech is in color and in music, in living forms of light resplendent. Here we speak and hear clumsy phrases, word symbols that express only a fragment of the thought we can formulate through the brain. But there no halting, articulated speech is needed, for mind speaks directly to mind, and matter is so subtle that every thought at once takes form.

If we pass into the devachanic world and think, the images of the thought spring up all around us. They flash in glorious colors, vivid and exquisite beyond all telling, delicate hues shading into one another in swiftly changing succession, inexpressibly fascinating. The more beautiful the thoughts, the fairer the forms; the greater and purer the ideas, the more exquisite the shapes that embody themselves as the radiant offspring of the mind.

All that we think is there before us. We think of a friend, and the image of our friend smiles upon us; we think of a place, and it lies stretched at our feet. Space cannot divide, for mind is not limited by space.

In the lower devachanic regions time is beginning to

yield, and past, present and future begin to melt into the now, though not yet wholly so. But we feel there the beginning of the blending which is perfected in loftier spheres.

When friends speak there, they speak in form and color and music, and the world around them is richer for it as its wondrous matter follows the vibrations of their thought.

Thus all the region of devachan is radiant with changing colors of which we on earth know nothing, musical with tones that physical ears cannot hear. There mere living is bliss ineffable, which nothing evil or inharmonious can disturb. No note of discord can pass into that world, for thought which cannot frame itself in harmony and beauty can find no expression. Each changing form seems fairer than the last, each tone fuller, sweeter, richer than the one before it. If everyone in a lecture hall had the devachanic senses awakened and functioning, then before words could fall from the speaker's lips, the whole room would seem full of music and color and form, the exquisite vesture of thought. Every sense would be stimulated and delighted at once, for all senses there are but one.

If we ask more closely as to the activities that belong to devachan, and how people will function in that lofty region when they become self-conscious there, again we must look to experience for the answer. We must examine the experience of those who have outrun their fellows and are already familiar with many devachanic powers and possibilities.

Service there takes on a new aspect, for as mind touches mind the lesser comes into direct contact with the Great Ones—as far as the lesser can touch the greater. The knowledge these beings impart is so full, so rich, that as it is studied new possibilities seem always to be welling up within it, and what is told is not a hundredth part of what is placed within reach. It seems to encircle and penetrate the mind till learners are plunged into a sea of wisdom and knowledge which permeates them through and through.

There again compassion expands, rejoicing in the new channels which it finds for its outward flowing.

Those on the devachanic plane reach downwards to all planes, sending down the forces that belong to those higher regions, to strengthen and illuminate peoples' minds. This influences masses instead of people one by one, affecting numbers by far-reaching thoughts, helping them to see truth as true, and impressing on the inner mind that which the outer brain is unable to comprehend.

Thus part of the help given to those who are aided consists in working on the inner or higher mind, suggesting a new idea, a scientific "discovery," a missing link of knowledge. This higher mind grasps the presented truth and works it into its own lower nature. This innermost conviction over-powers all logic and the slow processes of reasoning, illumi-nating the lower mind. It makes the thought comprehensi-ble and dominates the will, until all the lower nature is enlightened by the ray from its higher Self.

That is part of the help rendered by those who have reached the devachanic region, and it will be rendered more and more fully to the backward of the race as larger num-bers learn to function on the devachanic plane. It opens possibilities as yet hardly dreamed of: training thought to reach unimagined heights; making mighty elementals* and sending them forth to aid in the world; guiding minds grop-ing after truth; breathing loftiest inspirations into those who have fitted themselves to receive them. As thought takes form and the forces of devachanic life are thrown into it, such forms become a most potent agent, so that one worker can aid myriads.

Wisdom is so different on the devachanic level that it is scarcely possible to give even a glimpse of its methods and workings. It consists not in observing bodies, but in under-standing essences, not in observing effects, but in under-standing causes. Wisdom there sees and hears and knows; it deals with the causes of things instead of results, with the things themselves instead of their appearances. When the devachanic plane is reached, humanity will have vision reaching forward into the future, creating causes which will be worked out in following centuries. Help in evolution will

---

*Elementals are invisible forces of nature on the astral and other planes. They can be influenced to produce various effects.—ED.

then pour in from every side. The majority, instead of hindering progress, will forward it, instead of making obstacles, will lift those who are backward over them, for they will understand the divine Law and become coworkers with it in the progress of the world.

See how the sides of the pyramid seem to approach each other as we climb upwards, and love and wisdom blend their activities. So also with power. From what has been said, you can see the kind of power that then will be in the world, and how it will quicken evolution. For to have power on the devachanic plane is to be a fuller expression of the Good Law, a deeper channel for its mighty current. Perfect execution of Law is guided by perfectly rationalized obedience; each is the Law in action and is therefore overwhelming in strength. Now we go so slowly from century to century, from millennium to millennium. If we look back millions of years we see the human race still climbing on its way. But then progress will be enormously swifter. Obstacles will be a memory of the past, and all forces will be working consciously towards a fulfillment that is divine.

The Realm of Samadhi

Humanity must rise still higher. Beyond the glorious devachanic world opens yet another more glorious, the region of Samadhi, where a few of our race can function, though it is utterly unknown to the vast majority. It is a region where thought entirely changes its character and no longer exists as what is called thought on the lower planes. Consciousness loses many of its limitations, and acquires a new and strange expansion. Consciousness still knows itself to be itself, and yet has widened out to know other selves as one with it, so that it also includes the consciousness of others. It lives, breathes, feels with others, identifying itself with others, yet knowing its own center. It embraces others and is one with them, and yet at the same time remains itself. No words can express it; to be known it must be experienced.

This great expansion gives a hitherto unknown unity. The divisions of earth are lost, for we are nearing the center and looking outwards, thus feeling the oneness, instead of dwelling on the circumference and seeing the multiplicity. All that has been felt of service to those above us and compassion to those below us takes a new aspect, foreshadowing a yet more perfect unity. This is the unity of those who are higher and, because they are higher, realize their oneness with all below, seeing humanity in the unity of its spiritual nature instead of in the diversity of its material manifestations. Then compassion flows out, that compassion that sees and knows itself in every human soul, that understands all and therefore is able to help all. It feels with all and therefore is able to raise all. In the worst and most degraded it still realizes the possibilities that to it are actualities, as it sees in all people what they are in reality, not in appearance. This vision sees people as they will be (as we should say) in the future, which they eternally *are* in the eyes of those who know.

At this level, incomprehensible problems find simple solution, and things that seem unknowable come within the limits of the knowable. Disciples, rising higher and higher, find wisdom more far-reaching, power mightier, love more all-embracing, till even to the freed spirit it seems as though there could be no higher climbing, no greater possibilities to be realized.

Nirvana

Then before the awakening soul unfolds a yet mightier world which dwarfs all that went before. One more range is still within the limits of their vision—within the reach, not of human thought, but to some extent of human apprehension. Nirvana binds up all these glories of humanity. Its possibilities are seen and realized, and are no longer mere lovely dreams. They include life beyond all fancy of living, activity in wisdom and power and love beyond any wild imaginings, mighty hierarchies of spiritual Intelligences, each seeming vaster and more wonderful than the one before. What seems life on earth is but as death compared with that life; our sight is but blindness and our wisdom but folly.

What has humanity to do in such a region? What place has humankind in such a world as that?

And then, sweeping as it were from the very heart of it all —from the Logos who is its Life and Light—comes the knowledge that this is the goal of our pilgrimage, that this is our true home, that this is the world to which we really belong. All the gleams of light that have shown upon us in our weary journey have come from here. Then it comes into the dazzled consciousness that we have been living, experiencing and climbing from the physical to the astral, from the astral to the devachanic, from the devachanic to the samadhic, from the samadhic to the nirvanic for this end. We see that we might at last find ourselves in the Logos whence we came, that we might know his consciousness as the reflection of That, a ray from That.

The end of this stage of this mighty evolution—for there is no final end—is that each in turn should be the new Logos of a new universe, the perfect reduplication of the Light from which we came, to carry that Light to other worlds, to build from it another universe. That which awaits us is that mighty growth into a god, when we shall be the source of new life to others, and bring to other universes the Light which we ourselves contain.

But what words can tell of that vision, what thought, even flashing from mind to mind, may hope to give the faintest image of that which shall be? This sketch must be faint and imperfect. Only those before whose eyes have been unrolled the vast reaches of the untrodden vistas of those unborn years can know how faint and imperfect the sketch is. Yet it is a sketch, however dim, of the future which awaits us—a ray, however shadowy, of the glory that shall be revealed.

Sources

Chapter 1: A lecture delivered in the City Temple, London, October, 1907.

Chapter 2: *Theosophical Review*, May and June, 1899.

Chapter 3: Source unknown.

Chapter 4: A lecture delivered in 1895.

Chapter 5: *Theosophical Review*, October, 1897.

Chapter 6: *Theosophical Review*, May, 1900.

Chapter 7: *Theosophical Review*, February, 1900.

Chapter 8: *Theosophical Review*, January, 1906.

Chapter 9: An address given at the Parliament of Religions, Chicago, 1893.

Chapter 10: An address given at the Parliament of Religions, Chicago, 1893.

Chapter 11: A lecture given in India in 1894 or 1895.

Chapter 12: *Theosophical Review*, December, 1897.

Chapter 13: *Theosophical Review*, July, 1906.

Chapter 14: *Theosophical Review*, April, 1905.

Chapter 15: An address given to the London Lodge of the Theosophical Society, November, 1895.

We publish books on:

Healing and Health ● Occultism and Mysticism ● Transpersonal Psychology Philosophy ● Religion ● Reincarnation, Theosophical Philosophy ● Yoga and Meditation.

Other books of possible interest include:

Beyond the Post-Modern Mind *by Huston Smith*
Revised edition reviews latest ideas in science and theology.

East Meets West *edited by Rosemarie Stewart*
Our higher nature and transpersonal psychological implications.

From Atom to Kosmos *by L. Gordon Plummer*
Astronomy's stupendous universe theory relates to mysticism.

Fullness of Human Experience *by Dane Rudhyar*
How cyclic nature of creation affects our psychic evolution.

Inner Adventures *by E. Lester Smith*
Eminent scientist probes limits of thought and intuition.

Rhythm of Wholeness *by Dane Rudhyar*
We are part and parcel of the wholeness that always is.

The Theatre of the Mind *by Henryk Skolimowski*
The scope and importance of our evolution.

Two Faces of Time *by Lawrence W. Fagg*
Comparative study of time as viewed by religion and science.

The Wholeness Principle *by Anna Lemkow*
U. N. economist shows how all life is interdependent and unitive.

Available from:
The Theosophical Publishing House
P. O. Box 270, Wheaton, Illinois 60189-0270

Arsha Ware
617-732-5500

www.seethedoor.com

Kim
508-360-1275

501-739-6265

Oct 11 - 62 peak - M
Amelie - 236

236
62
———
298

941
733

49
500
298
———
202